Copyright © 2022 by Daejanggan Publisher
5-84, Maejukheon-ro 1176, Gayagok-myeon,
Nonsan, CN, South Korea
https://daejanggan.org
Printed in South Korea

Originally published in Korean under the title [평화, 그 아득한 희망을 걷다] in South Korea in 2012 by IVP Korea.

All rights reserved. No part of this publication may be reproduced, stored in a retrieval system, or transmitted in any form or by any means without the publisher's prior written permission. If you would like permission to use material from the book (other than for review purposes), please contact **jlife@daejanggan.org**.

Names: Song, Kang Ho, author.
Title: Peace, journeying into that distant hope / Song Kang Ho;
translated by Hugh Woonggul Park and Paco Michelson
ISBN: 978-89-7071-593 03330
Subjects: Pacifism – Religious aspects – Christianity | Peacemaking | Justice | War | Human rights | Korea

Cover Design: Minseo Park
Editor: Hakjoon Ko
Publisher: Yongha Bae

Price: 12,000 KRW | $10 U.S.

PEACE, JOURNEYING INTO THAT DISTANT HOPE

Song Kang Ho's Peace Narrative from Rwanda to Gangjeong

Song Kang Ho

Translated by by Hugh Woonggul Park & Paco Michelson

Editor's Note: For the sake of peace, Song Kang Ho threw his body to the roaring Gangjeong sea and was thrown behind bars. This book is a record written with every limb of his body. Parts One and Two are composed from in-depth interviews that took place in March 2012, right before his imprisonment in Jeju Island, South Korea. Part Three is primarily composed of letters and journal entries Song wrote in prison.

Note to the readers of the English edition: The names of Korean persons in this book are written in Korean name order: family name (usually one word, eg. Song) followed by given name (usually two words, eg. Kang Ho).

This book is dedicated, with my respect and love,
to the peace warriors who called me to Gangjeong village:
Kim Jong Hwan, Yang Yoon Mo and Choi Sung Hee.

From what I have observed, Dr. Song Kang Ho is a person who truly lives and acts out his faith.

-Fr. Moon Jeong Hyeon, a.k.a. "The Street Priest"

As Lu Xun put it, "We do not walk forward because we have hope, but because we walk forward, we have hope." In these times of desperation, when we cannot see the road ahead, and when our hearts and the heart of God break over and over, someone walks forward to overcome this deep sorrow. He is a stable friend of Gureombi Rock, and his name is Song Kang Ho.

-Gong Ji Young, Author of *Musical Chairs*

A man of prayer, warrior, dreamer, peacemaker, summons of conscience, watchman, and cornerstone. These are the images of Song Kang Ho that are imprinted in my mind after reading this book. A person who has accepted a life destined for endless defeat, yet someone who finds joy looking ahead to the victory of God. A person standing in the wilderness warning of the dangers of a faith not tested by hardship, and also a nomad who finds his home in every place where peace has collapsed. And now, God is restoring the church in Korea through him.

-Rev. Kim Ki Seok, Senior Pastor of Cheongpa Church

Last summer, I visited Gangjeong village. I saw the broken Gureombi Rock and the lives of many good people. I could never understand why it had to be this way. It was hard to see any hope, but someone was opening a path towards peace in these difficult circumstances. That person was Dr. Song Kang Ho. He was a person of peace and evidence of hope.

-Kim Mi Hwa, Broadcaster and Host of CBS Radio

The wind blows. I thought it was a gentle breeze that I could perhaps block with my hands. This wind, however, has become the mighty history of Gangjeong village on Jeju Island. When the divine breath permeates the body, you don't fear, and you don't tire. Wherever Song Kang Ho treads, that place soon becomes a fortress of peace. His every step forward makes flowers bloom again. Where the cold ocean waves used to rush in and crash over Gureombi Rock, Song Kang Ho stands tall, waving a majestic flag. With his presence, we never despair.

-Professor Kim Min Woong, Sungkonghoe University

As I shook hands with him, I thought to myself, 'It will be a long wait until I can grasp these hands again because he is fighting for the freedom of others at the expense of his own.' He is now crying out to us from prison. How great and beautiful freedom must be to one who has given up his own freedom. This book contains the story of his long journey toward freedom.

-Byun Sang Wook, Head of Content, CBS

CONTENTS

Foreword by Lee Hong Jung • 13
Foreword by Kwang Sun David Suh • 16
Acknowledgements • 17
Acknowledgements for the English Edition • 20

Prologue
Chapter 1 • Our Raggedy Hero, Song Kang Ho • 25
Chapter 2 • Jeju, the Island of Peace, and Gangjeong Village • 32

Part I
Chapter 3 • Conversion, the Beginning of a Voyage Towards Peace • 39
Chapter 4 • From Heidelberg to Rwanda • 49
Chapter 5 • Young People Crossing Snow-Capped Mountains • 60
Chapter 6 • Opening Peace School • 66

Part II
Chapter 7 • Gureombi, the Sacred Living Rock • 79
Chapter 8 • God's Calling • 89
Chapter 9 • Naval Base and the Island of Peace • 96
Chapter 10 • He Is Just Where He Should Be Right Now • 104

Part III
Chapter 11 • God's Hope Begins When We Become Hopeless • 113
Chapter 12 • Letters and Journals from Prison • 144
Chapter 13 • Man Named Song Kang Ho • 187

Epilogue
Voyage Towards Peace • 195

APPENDIX • 204

Peace as the Foundation of All Life-Giving Existence

Rev. Lee Hong Jung,

General Secretary of the National Council of Churches in Korea

The history of eco-justice and peace symbolized by Gureombi Rock was destroyed by the empire's anti-peace geopolitical strategy and power in the course of the construction of the Jeju Gangjeong Naval Base. As this storeroom of ancient memories of ecological history was blown up, the layers of the hearts of the Jeju people in which streaks of life were engraved and accumulated were irreparably cracked. Gureombi serves as an opportunity to reflect on the lesson that the totality and wholeness of peace are only possible when the strings of various relationships, woven into the web of life, create a justice of circulation with the spirituality of interdependence and self-emptying. Through Gureombi we also meet Dr. Song Kang Ho, who has lived as a center of the peace movement.

The world that Dr. Song Kang Ho sees is a world that is advancing toward peace. He experiences with his whole body the reality where knots of conflict-old, gnarled knots in the web of life create numerous distortions. They put today's peace into chaos and lock tomorrow's peace in ambiguity. However, he does not give up his ontological belief that the world is still on the road toward peace. For him, peace is the source of hope that enables the existence of the world, so it is a natural ontological consequence to live here and now as a being that builds peace.

Dr. Song Kang Ho is not an instigator who dreams of becoming the final resolution of the conflict. He participates in the scene of the conflict and plays a role in helping those who suffer to stand as subjects of peace building. In this process, he internalized a high-level receptivity; he has developed simple and clear judgment and cultivated the courage to practice nonviolent peace action. He shows that peace is realized through the power of solidarity, and solidarity begins with the voluntary practice of those who hear the voice of heaven in the reality of those who suffer.

The stories in this book are by themselves the events that make peace. Dr. Song Kang Ho's agony and reflection on ontological peace, the formation of solidarity, participation and action at the site itself, and the resulting years of hardship, unfold as stories in a loop of hermeneutic cycles. His beliefs and messages about peace shine the most from his period in prison. Prison life is not simply a time and place for physically restraining controlling peace action, but also for building a deeper inner peace, designing dreams for peace, and delivering the simplest and clearest message of peace toward an anti-peace world.

I hope, through this book, everyone who lives in a place of life longing for peace is awakened to an existence of peace. They will join the solidarity of peace in search of their own path so that events of peace may rise all over the world like active volcanoes. Peace is not created by entrusting power to presidents, generals, and state systems. Peace is possible through the but by each collective intelligence through acquiring the spirituality and strategy of peace that the Earth's life community has accumulated. We, along with the world, will continue our pilgrimage to peace until Gureombi Rock is transformed into token of peace for everyone. Peace is the foundation of all life-giving existence.

Dr. Song Kang Ho

Kwang Sun David Suh

Professor emeritus of Theology, Ewha Womans University

Dr. Song Kang Ho's letters from the 21st century Korean prison are in the long tradition of followers and disciples of Jesus. As a dangerous political prisoner against Pax Romana, St. Paul's letters to the Ephesians, Philippians, Colossians and Philemon were written from Roman prisons. Dr. Song's letters from prison to his wife reminds us of Dietrich Bonhoeffer's letters from Nazi prison to his fiancée, and Martin Luther King's "Letter from Birmingham Jail." We can also list numerous Christian political prisoners who fought more recently against military dictatorships for the democracy of Korea. Dr. Song writes, "Peace causes trouble for me…Was it a curse for me to dream of a world with no war?… I feel pain, but at the same time, joy. Maybe, my longing for peace is both a blessing and a curse." I hope he will be comforted and blessed by the words of Jesus: "Blessed are the peacemakers: for they shall be called the children of God." (Matthew 5:9)

Acknowledgements

This book started from an unexpected visit to Gangjeong by Kim Seong Han, when he and his colleagues suddenly pulled out a camera and started interviewing me. Kim Seong Han is a child-like person who loves for bicycles and music, and this book is purely a product of our friendship.

Initially, the completion and publication of this book seemed a bit adrift. However, through the editing efforts of Kim Jin Hyeong at IVP Korea, this book came together and finally reached completion. He reviewed, carefully read, and neatly edited together all the interview transcripts conducted in the spring just prior to my arrest, all my published articles from "The Frontiers" magazine, and the journal and letters written during my time in captivity.

I had assumed Yu Ga Il might have been disappointed by and even hostile to my extreme actions, but she surprised me by contributing Chapter One of the Prologue of this book where she called me a "raggedy hero." I was stunned to be called "hero" for the first time in my life. I am grateful for her contribution despite her busy Peace School work. My special thanks go to Han Jung Ae for organizing and collating all the articles that I have written for various publications. I am also grateful to film director Cho Sung Bong. He kindly provided most of the photos within this book. Additionally, film director Jeong Woo Cheol and photographer Lee Ji Hoon provided two very special photos that contained the spirit of Gureombi Rock. I am also thankful to the publishing house IVP Korea for their decision to publish a book on the theme of peace, which many Christians and their churches tend to neglect.

The Sitz im Leben (place in life) where these stories take place is Gangjeong village on the southern coast of Jeju Island, Korea. It was there that I was deeply moved by the villagers who had been fighting for peace for six long years. I am learning the truths of life from them. They are the real heroes in this era of violence and war.

There are many who live actively for peace in Gangjeong. To name a few, I am deeply thankful to Fr. Moon Jeong Hyeon, Bae Jong Ryul and Kwon Sool Yong. To many of us, they are like our fathers in faith and life. Despite adversity, they have led us on the path of peace throughout their lives, and they have become a signpost for all of us who follow in their footsteps. In addition, the dedication of Gureombi-protecting "Hoodlum of Justice" Yang Yun Mo and "Crazy Peace Lady" Choi Sung Hee has become the foundation for my Gangjeong story. I would also like to thank the village Mayor Kang Dong Gyun and Anti-Base Committee Chairman Koh Kwon Il for their wonderful leadership in the midst of our struggles.

I'd like to express my ardent gratitude to my lively and creative brothers and sisters of "SOS"(Save Our Seas) who I met in Gangjeong. My encounter with these romantic peace activists strengthened my inspiration and dream for my voyage towards peace. I also want to express particular gratitude to the members of The Frontiers community, the heroes that have granted me a life of peace. They are the real main characters in these stories.

Last but not least, I would like to thank my wife, Jeong Rae, from the bottom of my heart. From very early on, she has shared with me the pain and joy of dreaming and building a peace community together. My life for peace would have been impossible without her love and support. Also, to my dear children, Han Byeol and Saem, who will be delighted to hear that this book has been published. I want to express my gratitude to these children who supported the peace movement of their poor father and are proud of an imprisoned father.

Song Kang Ho

From Jeju Prison on the Demilitarized Island of Peace
September 12, 2012

Acknowledgements for the English Edition

I was in prison when the Korean version of this book was first published. Since then, I have been imprisoned several more times and am still in prison at this point, ten years later. It is punishment for my sin of dreaming of a world without militaries or war. But even in prison, I'm happy. Isn't it fun to live following in the footsteps of those that revealed peace, like the prophets Isaiah and Micah, or our Lord Jesus Christ?

A world without soldiers or war will never come to pass in our generation. However, not only do I think it is possible to drive out the military forces occupying our village and turn it into a peace park, but I also believe this is the duty of Christians living in the area. In the past decade, the biggest changes we have experienced worldwide were the COVID-19 pandemic and the ongoing climate disaster. Even in the midst of these crises, Northeast Asian countries (China, Japan, and the Koreas) are increasing defense spending and stockpiling weaponry. The military and its soldiers are one of the most vulnerable groups during a pandemic situation and are helpless to protect the lives and safety of the people during the climate disaster. In addition, militaries increase global warming through enormous, unnecessary high-density carbon emissions. War is nothing short of a mass suicide that destroys our endangered planet, but the world still cannot escape the specter of militarism.

This book is the story of my life for peace. It all began with prayer. Like a mustard seed, the first step in creating a peaceful world without war is always tiny. It starts with simple practices such as one-person demonstrations, letter writing, and ribbon wearing. I hope that readers of this book will take such a step. It is my wish that this hope will travel and spread beyond borders, so I am happy that this book has been translated into English. I am deeply grateful to Rev. Seo Seong Hwan for planning and promoting the English edition from the very beginning, and to the translators Rev. Hugh Park and Paco Michelson for their wonderful work. I thank all who worked for the release of this English edition: Rev. Lee Geun Bok, Rev. Hwang Pil Kyu, Rev. Son Eun Jeong, Rev. Han Myeong Seong, Rev. Lim Kwang Bin, Professor Han Guk Il, and all the members of The Frontiers community.

Song Kang Ho
Jeju Prison, Korea
September 11, 2021

Prologue

"The flag hung at the Joongdeok Three-Way Intersection, the base of the struggle, depicts a portrait of a man named Song Kang Ho."

Chapter 1

Our Raggedy Hero, Song Kang Ho

Yu Ga Il (Peace Activist)

I have always had uncomfortable feelings about Song Kang Ho, so I admit that writing about him does not come without worry. I first met him in the summer of 2003. The international peace organization "The Frontiers" used a space at the church I was attending at the time to hold a 'Prayer Meeting for the World' every Monday. Occasionally, there were posters recruiting participants for their Peace Camp in East Timor, but as I was then interested in working in the Islamic world, I didn't think much about it. I was in Iraq just before the war erupted in 2003, but returned briefly to Korea to recruit additional volunteers. And that's when I met him. Back in Iraq on the way the Baghdad, I ran into a team from The Frontiers by chance. They had just been robbed of their money and cameras. I remember thinking they seemed so disorganized and reckless. For the next few years, I basically forgot about Song Kang Ho and The Frontiers.

Meeting Him Again in Gangjeong

In July of 2011, after three and half years abroad, the first news I heard after my return to Korea was about Song Kang Ho's detention. Shocked, I rushed to Gangjeong, but his visitations were fully booked for the day so I couldn't meet him. However, the next day, he appeared with a sudden "Tada!" at the evening Candlelight Festival by the Gangjeong stream. But he was no longer the same soft and quiet Song Kang Ho that I remembered. To my surprise, he had transformed into a fighter.

The day after Korean Liberation Day was also the D-day of a large-scale police operation to clear out the protesters at the naval base construction site at Gangjeong. That same day was also the first day of The Frontiers' Jeju Peace Camp program. Cho Hyeon Oh, the Chief of the Korean National Police Agency, made a sudden visit to the Seogwipo Police Station and soon after, a massive police force from the mainland was deployed at Gangjeong village. The mainland police were an object of terror for the villagers.[1] Fortunately, by some miracle, the police crackdown was

---

1 Note to English Readers: The residents of Jeju were victims to extreme military/police brutality during the '4.3 Uprising,' when military, police, and para-military forces from mainland Korea killed roughly 10% of the Jeju population between 1948~1954 during its 'anti-rebel operations'. More than 90% of the villages in the mountainous regions of Jeju were destroyed and many of the casualties were women, children, and the elderly.

temporarily delayed. The next day I attended a lecture Song gave entitled, "Theory and Practice for Exciting Obstruction of Justice" and was so shocked and frightened that I left in the middle of the lecture. I was resistant to this, thinking, "That's too extreme! Why would we engage in obstruction of justice? We'll face arrest and imprisonment." I quit and left Peace Camp but stayed around Gureombi for a while.

Losing Gureombi, Starting a New Struggle

By the end of the month, official government notices regarding a court injunction against obstruction of construction were posted across Gangjeong. The notices named peace groups, residents, activists, and even the Gangjeong Village Association, stating that every attempt to enter the construction site or interfere with the naval base construction would result in a two million KRW fine per incident. Three days later, at dawn of September 2nd, the last open path to Gureombi Rock was blocked by more than 1,000 heavily armored riot police. The crackdown was violent, and the air was filled with screams. Thirty-five people were arrested and Gureombi was stolen from us.

It was from this moment onward, that Song Kang Ho's valuable light began to truly shine. As soon as the overland route to Gureombi was blocked, he recruited and formed a maritime action team. Before I had left the Peace Camp, activists from Okinawa, Japan had told stories about their kayak protests against the U.S.

military bases in Okinawa, but at the time I had doubted, "Would we really do that here?" However, Song, now nicknamed "Water Spirit", had gathered a team of activists with nicknames resembling the ingredients to a seafood stew: Squid, Tuna, Saury, and Dolphin, and they began to train and make practical plans to block the blast explosions of Gureombi and the sea dredging barges. During this time, people were being arrested daily for protesting at the main land gate to the naval base construction site.

Gureombi, Song's Place of Prayer

Later that summer, Song asked me why I had quit the Peace Camp and I replied with this excuse: "I didn't come here to fight or shout, I came to pray." But in actuality, I couldn't even breathe, let alone pray. I was suffocating from fear and constant sirens. However, it was Song who actually did pray. Every dawn, he went to Gureombi to pray. The following became his routine: swim to Gureombi, get assaulted by the navy, go through arrest and investigation, and finally be released again.

In October, during a session of the newly formed Gangjeong Peace School, Song stated, "We must set up courses from beginner through intermediate with the clear goal of training peace activists to be immediately able carry out on-the-ground peace work." As I had not studied or trained to be a peace activist, and only had a brief experience with the peace movement, this made my stomach hurt.

Although I didn't have much field experience, I agreed that the students at Peace School needed practical "front line" experience. So, I participated in maritime team training when weather conditions allowed. I can't forget the first time we made it back to the now forbidden Gureombi Rock for our first class right before it was surrounded with barbed wire. We monitored the construction site together with the other students. Song was repeatedly arrested during the Peace School. I still keep in my heart one of our visits to see him in detention at the Jeju Dongbu Police Station. He gave us an impromptu five-minute lecture, "Life, Peace, Justice, and God's Kingdom", and the room was full of tears.

Song Kang Ho often left me with feelings of both shame and awe. When an offshore dredging barge appeared in Gangjeong on January 26, he jumped in the water to swim towards it, and was immediately arrested. In March, when 1.5 tons of explosives were placed to blast Gureombi, he and the maritime activist team launched a literal guerrilla-style sea operation to stop the blasting. Around a dozen members of the maritime team wrestled against the Coast Guard across the Gangjeong coast, but the blasting was still carried out. Still, when I saw that Song and few others were able to enter Gureombi in the midst of the chaos, I felt some shame and thought, "Wow, he's like the Terminator. I can't do something like that."

Our Raggedy Hero

Even today, banners of Song waving an anti-naval base flag hang from the town hall and the tall watchtower at the Joongdeok Three-Way Intersection. But no one there calls him a hero. If he is a hero, he is a shabby and ragged hero, a bloody hero who is beaten daily, a hero who no one can easily follow, nor wants to follow, an uncomfortable hero. No matter how gilded a cross may be, it is still a symbol of the gallows. Song Kang Ho's banners are similar. They hang as a symbol that is easier to turn a blind eye to, than to revere.

On Palm Sunday during the Holy Week, as Song was violently arrested on Gureombi, I was arranging pictures of activists injured by police in Gangjeong. Next to pictures of a bruised hand hit with a hammer, a forehead cut open by a camera, and a picture of Song "bleeding and lying there like the dead", I placed a picture of Jesus bleeding from his crown of thorns and attached this prayer, "Fill our bodies with the suffering of the Lord. The tears have become our daily bread."
Walking the Dangerous Path

Song's writings and words are as straightforward as he is. They are like official statements from someone who has completed his own set of values as well as a belief system. He is always ready to die for what he believes, and he cannot be shaken. He will one day breathe his last in a "conflict area" like this (Yes, it's a terrible thing to say but that's what he wishes for himself). In fact, he has already faced several 'Well, this must be it' situations in Gangjeong. Those that are prepared to die are not conflicted. Sometimes, this can be difficult for those like me, who hesitate and fall behind.

Simply put, he is an example of radical Christian societal participation. Even among fellow Christians he is not just misunderstood but attacked. Yet he continues to walk his precarious path. In the midst of suffering, he remains in the powerful grip of God where he experiences, "the Lord's secret peace that the world cannot give." His courage, perseverance, sacrifice, and hardships for the sake of justice are reminiscent of Jesus and his life. When you finish reading his story you may find yourself in the same dilemma as me. It is similar to reading the gospels. You must either decide to worship Jesus or reject him as a lunatic. Likewise, after reading this book, you will have to decide whether to follow Song on his path or turn from him. You will experience discomfort and internal conflict. You will be unable to step away and just "like and respect" Song.

Are you now afraid? Then you are ready for his story.

Chapter 2

Jeju, the Island of Peace, and Gangjeong Village

On the volcanic rock seaboard birthed by Mt. Halla sits Gangjeong, a remote Seogwipo village. A sorrowful gloom has been slowly engulfing this little village. The people of Gangjeong and Jeju Island are no strangers to such sorrow.

Jeju Island was dubbed the "Island of Peace" not long ago. In January 2005, The Roh Moo Hyun Administration designated Jeju as the "Island of World Peace" through Article 12 of the Special Act on the Establishment of Jeju Special Self-Governing Province and the Development of Free International City. The official "Jeju, Island of World Peace" website run by the Korean government defines 'peace' as follows:

> There are two perspectives to peace. One is passive and the other active. The passive perspective views peace as a state of no war, but one cannot expect a true lasting peace from this perspective. Thus, there is a need for a more active sense of peace. Active peace is not content with the

mere absence of war but seeks a state where all human basic needs are met, and justice prevails.

The Island of World Peace aims for "cultural, social and political activities that embrace a system of thinking and policy that practices the active sense of peace. It is a state free from every threat factor." This calls for a process that creates, expands and builds peace by forming intellectual, human, and material networks between members of society to realize this active sense of peace.

The context for the "Island of World Peace" designation is expounded upon further:

> Jeju has carried a custom of peace since ancient times with its traditional Sammu, or "Spirit of Three Absences": no thieves, no gates, no beggars. Jeju also carries a lingering Han sense of suffering from deep historical trauma, including the greatest tragedy in modern Korean history, the events of the 4.3 Uprising. The people of Jeju have overcome this sorrow, cherishing peace within their hearts.

The name "Island of Peace" reflects a fervent hope for peace. It contains the will to oppose war and the commitment to building a peace community through reconciliation and reparation of the wounds of the traumatic events of the 4.3 Uprising.[2]

---

[2] On March 1st, 1947, police opened fire on protesters demonstrating against the actions of the U.S. military occupation and its officials, which led to a broader civil resistance movement. The military administration responded with mass detention and torture, which

If you take Bus 600 from Jeju Airport, Gangjeong village is about an hour away. It has long been known as a peaceful community and good place to live, traditionally topping the list of southern Jeju islanders' good places to live: Gangjeong was called "Il Gangjeong" (No. 1 Gangjeong) or "Number One Gangjeong; nearby Hwasoon was second and called "I Beonnae" (No. 2 Village), and Shindo in Daejeong Eup was third and called "Samdowon" (No. 3 Place). In other words, "Il Gangjeong" was the best place to live.

After passing by houses with beautiful gardens of tangerine trees and walking towards the Gangjeong Harbor for about 10 minutes, you will come across a broad flat rock called "Gureombi" spread across the coastline. Gureombi rock is distinct from other types of rock structures seen across Jeju Island. It is a single, broad, flat rock stretching 1.2 km in length, with fresh spring water coming from deep under the rock, forming natural pools at the edge of the sea. It quenches the thirst of passers-by and provides a summer playground for children. Tan-faced haenyeo, or

---

led to the start of an armed uprising on April 3rd ("4.3"), 1948. When the Rhee Syngman government took power in the same year, martial law was declared on Jeju Island and a violent military crackdown ensued, killing countless innocent island residents. The situation continued in this manner until September 21st, 1954, with conservative estimates of at least 25,000-30,000 civilian, 180 military, and 140 police deaths. In the year 2000, the ROK Prime Minister chaired "National Committee for Investigation of the Truth about the Jeju 4.3 Events" was launched and on October 31st, 2003, then President Roh Moo Hyun acknowledged that large-scale sacrifices, at the expense of the Jeju people, were caused by the state's armed suppression of the Jeju Namro Party supported civilian resistance militia. President Roh issued an official apology to the surviving bereaved families and the residents of Jeju Island.

Jeju's traditional female divers, soak their tired bodies in these pools after laboring underwater.

Gureombi and its natural pools are also a bedrock wetland, providing safe homes to many endangered plants and wild animals such as the red-foot crab, the boreal digging frog, and the Jeju Saebaengi, a local fresh-water shrimp. If you briefly follow the Gangjeong Stream back up towards Mt. Halla, you will come across 'Naekirisoh', a breathtaking pond with clear emerald, blue water, enclosed by cliffs. The word 'Naekirisoh' indicates four things: "waterfall", "rock wall", the Eun-eo sweetfish and "clean water". The village children play here along with the sweetfish and spot-billed ducks. Back at the Gangjeong shore, you might be lucky enough to watch dolphins dance in front of nearby Beom Island.

However, tragedy again stirs in the once peaceful Gangjeong. In January of 2005, The Roh Moo Hyun government, ironically the same government which had previously declared Jeju the "Island of Peace", decided to build a naval base in Gangjeong. In April of 2007, the village mayor at the time agreed to the national government's plan with the support of only 87 village residents. Angered, a majority of residents voted to immediately remove that mayor from office and elected a new leader. In August of the same year, the villagers held a referendum on the base issue. Approximately 1400 of a total 1900 residents were over 18 (of voting age), with about 1050 residing in the village at the time. 725 of these village residents voted, with 680, or 94%, voting against the naval base construction. But this vote was in vain. The navy ignored the results and moved forward with their plan for construction, resulting in the current turmoil we see in Gangjeong to this day. The Korean National Assembly passed the budget for the construction by a hair in December of 2010 as part of the 2011 budget. The following February, the construction began and the struggle of Gangjeong residents and peace activists reached its peak.

At the Joongdeok Samgeori (Joongdeok three-way-intersection), there is a banner hung by residents with a painted portrait of Song Kang Ho. He opposes war, yearns for peace, and will fight for justice even at risk of loss of his own life. He has won the hearts of many in this community torn apart by the divisions caused by the naval base construction.

On April 1st, 2012, Song Kang Ho was violently arrested by the police after breaking into a barbed wire surrounded demolition site on Gureombi Rock. He was assaulted in the course of being taken to the police station leaving him with a chipped front tooth, a broken molar and wound on his chin requiring stitches. As if by destiny, Song was imprisoned on April 3rd, the anniversary of the start of the Jeju 4.3 Uprising in 1948.

How did he end up in Gangjeong? What does Gangjeong have to do with him? In response to these questions, Song began his story with his religious conversion into Christianity.

Part I

"Truth can be found through long pondering and reflection, but truthfulness is guaranteed by its simple and humble practice."

Chapter 3

Conversion, the Beginning of a Voyage Towards Peace

> *"Truth walks with the calmest demeanor
> while embracing the most convoluted reality."*
> -Park Noh Hae, "Facing the Decision"

Song Kang Ho started going to church at the age of 17 with some friends. At that time, he lived in Seoul by himself while his parents resided in Dongducheon, a city to the north of Seoul. He enjoyed going to church, but his father was not fond of religious belief and his grandmother preferred traditional Korean shamanism so going to church was not always easy for him. His church activities gradually made him serious about its teachings and strengthened his faith, but he struggled with the biblical account of the resurrection of Jesus, being unable to rationally understand it and struggling to accept or reject it. Although he could not fully understand the resurrection event, he eventually decided to accept it and transform from a church goer to a believer.

> "I came across a certain predicament as I started attending church. I believed that the 'resurrection event' was the line between a serious believer and a complete non-believer. I was having a hard time deciding to either accept Christ's resurrection as my own or totally reject it. Will I believe in the resurrection and that I too will be resurrected in a similar manner? Or will I say, 'Oh, this is a lie, Christianity is a ridiculous scam!' When thinking about refusing, it was difficult to ignore the vast reality of Christianity, but harder still to acknowledge this resurrection underlying it all. So, I kept hovering at that threshold, and at some point, I came to realize that Christianity cannot be fully explained rationally, cannot be proved, is beyond my own limited judgement, and it's simply a matter of deciding to believe or not. And I wanted to believe in this unacceptable thing. I think this yearning was the grace of God."

This is not often the case with most Christians. Although "resurrection" is generally a touchstone for most believers and they may say they believe in it, not many believers necessarily have complete faith in it. For Song however, his faith in Christ meant everything to him. And for him, it was impossible to become a Christian without being a disciple of Christ. He was that firm and resolute.

> "One thing I really couldn't understand was the word 'Lord.' It was

a very heavy word for me. I too wanted to be truly loyal to someone, to dedicate my entire life to a wonderful monarch. But then I wondered, so many churchgoers say, 'Lord…,' but do they really believe that with their lives? It occurred to me that two things are deceiving the church. One is eschatological. We believe that this world has an end, but actually live as if it will last forever, especially when it comes to our own or our families' interests. And our pastors live much the same. The second is this term, 'Lord.' We say it, but we don't truly live as servants. This reality of the church makes me cynical, 'Ah, the Church has just tacitly accepted a lie together and everyone lives as they wish.'"

A truly converted Christian cannot compromise their Christian reality. The Kingdom of God is against the values of this present world and seeks to overcome those values. How could someone committed to the values of God's Kingdom come to terms with the values of this current world? Song spent his youth wrestling with the essential issues of Christianity, such as the reality and meaning of the resurrection, reason, faith, repentance, and how to live as a devoted disciple. Initially he did not see a reason to go to college, and he wandered away from these questions for a time, but after eventually entering college, his search for truth picked up where he had left off. His search for a genuine faith led him to various Christian missionary organizations. But he was soon deeply disappointed with their excess focus on personal faith and evangelism. He sought real faith connected to the realities of the world, not mere zealotry. Questions regarding the historicity of the bible never left his mind. For Song, truth could never be reduced to just questions of reason. Rather, genuine truth is not simply what is correct, but that which awakens and consoles, and pushes us to journey onward.

When he entered seminary, he studied hard, trying to maintain his faith without turning away from academic challenges. However, he found theology vain in some respects. In seminary, a theology that deeply affected real people's lives and the realities of this world did not exist. He could not shake off the suspicion that denominations and special interest groups were using theological education as a kind of self-defense mechanism. Eventually he changed his focus and went to graduate school for education, as he had a great interest in deeply influencing people and changing lives.

"I was deeply disappointed with the church, and I developed an interest in pedagogy as a practical alternative. I chose philosophy of education in graduate school with the idea of organizing pedagogical knowledge of enlightenment. The title of my graduate thesis was 'The Pedagogical Anthropology of Enlightenment.' By studying this topic in such an academic manner, I wanted to help others like me, who struggled with understanding and reconciling various values. To have faith is to change one's entire worldview, values and whole identity. It's enormous work, greater than demolishing an old house and re-building a new one. I wasted my entire youth on these issues without sufficient help. Thus, I wanted to be a person who helps those who were wandering like me."

Song witnessed the sad reality that many Christians are quick to confess their faith in Christ, but do not demonstrate it in their everyday lives. This made him interested in the fundamental changes that occur in people's lives, which eventually gave birth to his academic interest in education. By extension, he also came to have a great interest in communities.

"I had a dream of a genuine Christianity and its true community since my time at the seminary. When I was a student, I saw Reverend Kim Jin Hong as a model in this regard after reading his book I Will Wake the Dawn. I loved his appealing talks. However, it was strange to me that most organizations were identified with one single person. For example, 'Doo Rae Community equals Kim Jin Hong' and 'L'Abri equals Francis Schaefer.' That didn't seem right to me. I sought a community model where all the members of the community grew together and envisioned the values of the community, and this later became the driving force behind the community, 'The Frontiers.'"

"The Frontiers" is now an international peace organization. The Frontiers started in 1991 when Song Kang Ho led a group of young people to the Philippines following the eruption of Mt. Pinatubo, a disaster that left 900 people dead and around 250,000 homeless.

He strongly desired for young Christians to work in the world and beyond the walls of the church. He thought it was the only way for young people to overcome their disappointments with the church and still identify as Christians. After the "Kang Kyeong Dae Incident"[1] in 1991, they made condolence ribbons to distribute to all their congregational members. They also started a social advocacy group among the youth to publicize social issues to their congregation. They sought to be genuine believers by embracing the wider world. For that, the Philippines was their first destination.

> "We visited various islands including Luzon, Solanu, Batangas and Mindoro in the Philippines. In Solanu, we encountered some members of the communist groups. The Pinatubo volcanic eruptions took place in the Angeles area where a U.S. air force base was also located. There we experienced a feeling of feebleness in the face of that devastating reality. All we did in the middle of such a disaster was some street performances asking people to believe in Jesus. It was like handing out boxes of chocolates with pretty ribbons to limb-sev-

---

1 In 1991, a Myongji University student named Kang Kyeong Dae, a participant in the student struggle against Government control over universities, was beaten and killed by the riot police who suppressed the demonstration. Later Myongji University placed a memorial copperplate on the wall where Kang Kyeong Dae fell.

ered and scar-faced victims of war, saying, 'Here's a treat for you!' We found ourselves to be completely out of touch with their reality."

Song was often frustrated to see many young people respond to his message by saying "Amen" while not changing anything in their lives. He wondered what energy might shake their worldviews from their roots. Having himself been shocked by the disaster in the Philippines, he realized that "The world can be our school."

"A school where the world is the classroom and God the teacher, a school that uproots each person's life from the bottom up with a personalized curriculum for each individual! This world, filled with not only the beautiful and brilliant Mother Nature but also the reality of the countless pains and agonies of life and death situations that people are facing, is the school. I am merely a guide that introduces the students to the school of the world, and God is the teacher who will change them eventually."

Knowing God cannot just remain a piece of knowledge. It inevitably requires a change in life. The reality of the world which we are standing on is critically important for that knowledge because God is always present with specific people in specific places. Where there are all kinds of diseases and disasters, poverty and injustice, suffering from conflict and war, anywhere where people are crying out, God is there with them.

"It looks like we have detained God within the walls of the church. This is an even greater sin than putting a person in prison. The church doesn't appear to be happy when their young people are eager to spend more time, materials, and attention on issues outside of the church than inside. This is what eventually gave birth to The Frontiers."

It was in these troubled places of the world where Song looked for paths forward for his interest in and dreams of education and community.

"As I was reading the Bible, I became more conscious of the suffering of the Israelites from war. One of the most miserable causes of death is hunger, and the problem of hunger, whether directly or indirectly, is largely a result of war. When a tsunami hit Banda Aceh, Indonesia in 2005, I was surprised to see the enormous aid capacities of major international relief organizations. However, tribal and ethnic conflicts made it difficult for such reliefs to reach the victims. This is one of the reasons why countries like Ethiopia and Sudan always face chronic hunger problems. If transportation routes for aid distribution were safe, the lives of many people dying from hunger and famine could be saved. But we are our own obstacle as the fundamental cause of hunger today is war, and war often springs from ethnic or racial conflicts. So obviously, our prayers began to change.

We used to pray for missionaries, but gradually we began to pray for the those experiencing poverty across the world and the conflicts at the roots of this poverty."

However, Song Kang Ho and his group of young people were no longer welcomed in their church. The church would not allow them to use its facilities for their gatherings, so they had to find a new venue for their prayer meetings. But they never stopped praying for the world. What does it mean to pray? If you are praying for someone and learn they are starving, shouldn't you give them some food? Likewise, they wanted to not only pray for conflict areas, but join those living there in these conflicts. It could be dangerous, but they were willing, and their passion was the soil from which The Frontiers grew.

"I don't think that the first priority of education is to just teach everyone how to be a fighter for justice and peace. Every individual has their own dreams from God and their own unique desires. Everyone longs for a happy life. Shouldn't the goal of education be to open the way for them to live their life in a truly free way? I think that's my role.

The reason I love the sea and encourage young people to sail is to give them a taste of how wide, free and wonderful the happiness they can enjoy and spread can be. By seeing the vastness of the world, I want them to realize the infinite nature of freedom and break away from the conventional wisdom and the prejudices and biases that lurk in their minds and hearts. Life is just like sailing. Like a sailboat riding rolling waves in unpredictable winds, we are sailing our lives on a sea of fate. Just as the sea does not conform to the plans of its navigators, we must continually learn to put down our stubbornness, modify our will, and change our determination in an ever-changing reality, appraising and affirming the present world around us as we move onward. That's why I ask them to go to the sea. I hope that young people can enjoy freedom but still live spirit-fully in the world without compromising against injustice. The reason you don't have a boat is because you don't have the sea in your heart."

Not only did he care for young people, he also lived wild and young-at-heart.

Chapter 4

From Heidelberg to Rwanda

There were many young students living in poor conditions in the Bokwang-dong area of Seoul where Song started his church youth group. Quite a few young people were addicted to sniffing glue in homes left unattended by parents. There was an incident where some teenagers accidently caused an explosion in an empty house that was filled with butane gas with lit cigarettes. One was killed and two suffered severe burns. One of the victims was a member of his church. Song was heartbroken. During weekdays, his church had many empty unused rooms, so he proposed a plan to the denomination head office to create a youth program for the wider community. However, the education department of the denomination rejected the proposal stating that they were too occupied preparing for summer bible school. The social affairs department also declined the proposal as they were too busy with their evangelism outreach efforts. Eventually, Song gave up on garnering support and tried to plan a program locally.

Two years later, the denomination head office contacted Song, encouraging him to apply for a scholarship program from the World Council of Churches for young leaders. Although they had not accepted his previous proposals, they now wanted to offer him an opportunity to study overseas. Song eventually accepted and headed to Heidelberg University. However, he could not push the youth of his church out of his mind, and so he made a promise with them.

> "As I said goodbye to the young adult group with whom I had spent three years together, I felt sorry that I hadn't quite finished the job of tackling the question 'How to live as Christians in the world.' However, I was confident that I had built strong relationships with them. So, I made a promise with them. 'If the most serious and urgent problems in the world are war and hunger, let us go there when they take place. Let us learn what the causes are, and experience what we could do in such a situation. We shall meet when a war arises.' Even still, I felt like a father abandoning his own children at an orphanage for a fancy opportunity in Germany."

The professors he met in Heidelberg taught him about scholarship. They roamed around the city on their bicycles with their old leather bags, white hair streaming in the wind. They sat on the library floor and passionately explored original texts and writings.

They engaged in informal discussions with students anytime, anywhere, and with no sense of authoritarianism. In Korea, some would disparage such radical scholars, but their fervor for truth greatly inspired Song.

"I wondered if those who would criticize such professors as 'neo-theologians,' 'higher critics,' or 'liberals' have ever so passionately explored the truth as the people they criticized have. I could not help but admire their attitudes as scholars. I thought, 'This is how you study!' When I was in Korea, I had a small bit of courage to teach young people to be Christians who respond to the challenges of the world as it is, but at the same time, I was somewhat ignorant and unprepared. An ignorant person with too much courage can really harm society. I worried that I might be such a person, you know, just randomly inciting the youth. If you're doing this kind of work you need to study and reflect carefully, but I hadn't yet laid such a foundation for myself. I was given an opportunity to organize my faith and theology, so I decided not to pass this opportunity too hastily or arrogantly, but to study prudently and with humility."

The topic of his dissertation was "conversion," but he was a bit worried that his progressive German professors might not be interested in such a topic. To his surprise, however, the supervising professor readily agreed and encouraged it.

"Initially, I told my professor that I wanted to write about Bonhoeffer's pedagogical views for my dissertation subject. The professor looked at me in silence for a moment before asking me what topic I was really interested in. As if I was drawing water from a deep well, very slowly and seriously, I said, 'Conversion.' He asked for my thoughts on conversion, so I explained, 'I'm still thinking it through, but I have experienced conversion along with some dramatic changes in my life, and I've come to learn that a true conversion is one of not just love for God but also love for people. Based on my experience and academic intuition thus far, this is the key to human change in his or her encounters with God. I think I can find evidence to support the idea that true conversion is only possible through meaningful interaction with our neighbors, with other people.' To my surprise, the professor liked the idea and asked me to write a short 40-page essay on it. Since it was based on my own story, I thought it was basically half-written already. I went home and celebrated with my wife."

"I've had two conversions in my life. The first was when I encountered Jesus Christ directly and the second was meeting God of Love through 'significant encounters' with 'meaningful others.' Loving God through Christ means loving others and this is not a one-off conversion event but an ongoing journey that occurs through the process of constant encounters. I saw that such an idea could be pedagogically explicated, just as James Fowler emphasizes the importance of 'meaningful others' in his book, *The Stages of Faith*."

Song's writing was progressing smoothly. Perhaps it was one of the most peaceful times of his life. However, this serene routine didn't last long. One spring day, two letters arrived. One was from the scholarship committee of the German Protestant Church that had originally invited him to Germany. It said they were interested in his dissertation topic. Around 10 percent of the German population at that time were Turkish, and there were quite a few Islamic fundamentalists among them who were often at odds with German conservative Christians. Many fundamentalist Christians in Germany were bound up with far-right racists nostalgic for Nazism and as a result German society was experiencing heavy social stratification. However, some philosophers, like Levinas, were stressing the significance of "the other" at the time. That first letter promised long-term sponsorship for Song's dissertation writing. Things appeared to be working out well, until the second letter doused his plans in cold water.

"Dear Pastor, a war has broken out! We remember that you used to say we would go together to a conflict zone in the event of war, so we are now discussing concrete action plans." In 1994, war broke out in Rwanda. With that letter in my hands, my life felt like it was turning again. Was I to give up my doctorate program to go support these young people and keep my promise to them? Or should I remain in Germany, concentrate on completing my dissertation first, and waiting for another war to arise? I didn't know how to respond, but I couldn't shake the thought, 'Isn't a promise a promise?' So, I wrote to the head of the scholarship committee: 'I am eager to start my dissertation writing. However, there is currently an ethnic conflict in Rwanda and if I had an opportunity to observe this issue personally it would be of significant academic value to my dissertation. I want to visit Africa.' The Committee replied, 'The German church has been selecting scholarships from all over the world for the last 150 years and we have never seen such a case before. But have a safe trip.' There was no clear indication of their continued sponsorship or not of my doctorate studies."

It was that simple for him. Truth can be found through long pondering and reflection, but truthfulness is guaranteed by its simple and humble practice. He quit in the spring semester of 1994 and headed to Africa in June of the same year. Song reunited with his young friends and confirmed their genuine friendship. Since the road to Rwanda was blocked, they first went to Bujumbura, the capital of Burundi, which was also a conflict zone at the time.

"Like Rwanda, Burundi had a similar ethnic population ratio between the Hutus and Tutsis. Thus, as the conflict in Rwanda between the groups reached its peak, Burundi also became a dangerous place. We were staying at a local missionary's home waiting for an opportunity to enter Rwanda. One day, we attended a prayer meeting led by a group of missionaries. The venue was in a Tutsi area and a few pastors from a Hutu region were also at the meeting. The hosting missionaries were Korean pastors from the U.S., and they preached about the story of the good shepherd from the Gospel of John Chapter 10. The Hutu pastors were filled with guilt and pain because they couldn't stop the conflict in their neighborhood and church elders and deacons were killing each other with knives and bamboo spears. As the sermon went on that evening, they could not bear the increasing sense of guilt that they had abandoned their own 'sheep.' Soon, the pastors fell to the floor, weeping bitterly.

As we were having dinner together following the tearful meeting, we heard gunshots all of a sudden. United Nations staff phoned us to warn that a massive Tutsi counterattack had just begun. Since the next day was Independence Day, they were concerned about our safety. The local pastors warned the Korean missionaries of the danger and they wondered if they should go back to their local church or stay in the Tutsi area for the night."

The situation was dangerous, but we thought that maybe since we were foreigners, we could be of some help to them as a sort of human shield. In the middle of our fervent prayers, a woman stood up and announced prophetically: 'God does not want us to go tonight, instead we have a role to play here in earnest prayer.' We decided to accept her prophetic suggestion. That night I couldn't sleep. I spent the night thinking about Chapter 10 from the gospel of John, about working for peace, and how close death might be for us.

Fortunately, everyone in that Tutsi area were safe that night. However, the memory of that night seared Song's heart like a scar. For peace, he knew he must endure all kinds of violence and risk, but that night he had trembled in the face of death. The Hutu and Tutsi were divided against each other and they both slaughtered anyone who dared otherwise. Witnessing with his own eyes one of the worst human tragedies, Song thought he should gather young people from around the world. He believed that if he could gather as many young people as he could from various countries, they could be trained to defuse such situations as third parties and hopefully prevent terrible tragedies. The memory of that painful sleepless night brought him some hope.

Those "significant encounters" with "meaningful others" in Rwanda provided him with the exact second conversion experience that was the topic of his dissertation. Such encounters can leave frustration and scars, but through proper reflection and perseverance, new hope can sprout. More importantly, ontological change was possible through such encounters, which is what happened to Song and his young friends. Throughout his entire peace ministry, it was more of such "significant encounters" like Peace Camp, Peace School, and the Gangjeong struggle that became important driving forces for his conversion.

Since the road to Rwanda was still blocked, they took a detour toward the Tanzanian border through Kampala, the Ugandan capital, where they stayed at a refugee camp situated in the Kagera River Basin on the border of Rwanda. Within the camp, only a dozen U.N. staff took care of about 50,000 refugees. The HIV infection rate in Uganda and Tanzania was reportedly over 30 percent at the time. A single village was said to have been annihilated completely by HIV infections alone. When food rations were handed out twice a day, all the residents of the camp, from young to the elderly, had to line up under the hot scorching sun for hours. Some U.N. staff would beat back swarming children with whips. Young girls walked along miles of dusty road to fetch water from a swamp. When night fell the children and adults would gather to sing. An adult would sing the phrase, "Pick out the eyes of the Tutsi," and the children would respond, "Chew them up." Extreme hate and anger permeated this camp where there seemed to be no future.

"I didn't expect there to be a school in the refugee camp, but there was a school in that camp. However, it was not a school preparing for the future, but a school bound by the past. The teachers gathered children every night to sharpen the sword of revenge and hatred. One evening, I asked a young man if they might teach a song about peace and reconciliation with the Tutsi for the sake of the children. Suddenly, I felt every eye of the youth turn on me, pupils blazing in darkness. It was a murderous look. I backed away and ran to the U.N. staff tent site. Back in my tent, my heart still pounded, and I couldn't sleep. I stayed up all night thinking about that terrible school of war and violence.

When I opened my eyes in the morning, I could see the children lining up again at the foot of the mountain for food, and the girls carrying the water buckets. Middle-aged men in ragged clothing chewed drugs and gambled on the roadside. Bored sex workers laughed together nearby. A thought crossed my mind. "Let's put up a big white tent here to start a school for peacebuilding for these children. Let's appeal to young people in other countries who feel some responsibility to respond to war. Let's stop this war, break the chain of revenge and hatred and make peace. Let's call the young people of the world to teach peace to these children!" I saw an image of children running up the mountain at the sound of a school bell. My heart pounded with the excitement of hope. It was only a daydream, but I've kept it in my heart as it felt like a vision from God."

In the middle of war, revenge, and hatred, Song Kang Ho was dreaming of a school for peace.

"Peace School will send a message to society, 'You have a future, too!' Living without a future, one has no choice but despair. A society without a future pushes its people to extremes as they grab onto whatever power and material goods they can grasp in the moment. Once a society and its members realize that they have a future, they have no choice but to abandon conflicts and disputes between each other and seek peace. That's how the dream of holding peace camps and establishing peace schools in conflict areas began."

Peace is a flower that often blooms out of the flames of conflict. No one would look for it in earnest in a place of peace. Life and death, joy and worry, and love and hate; they are usually together. This is what the journey of life is like from the beginning. It is the "possibility of the impossible."

-Ham Seok Heon, "Let Us Make a Peace Movement"

Chapter 5

Young People Crossing Snow-Capped Mountains

Song Kang Ho also travelled to Somalia and Bosnia. Somalia was in a state of chaos, with continuous conflicts between local tribes and military warlords in collusion with European imperialist foreign powers. Bosnia was similarly being devastated by religious exclusivity, violence and destruction.

"Someone once said, 'If an ordinary person is doing evil, there must be religion involved.' That's true. Even good people can do evil if religion is involved. Religion can turn evil people towards what is good, but paradoxically, it has the power to make good people do evil. After Hutu extremists in Rwanda slaughtered many members of the Tutsi community, pilling up a mountain of dead bodies, they praised God for God's help in their bloody victory. Ninety percent of the Rwandan population was Christian at that time. During the Crusades, Christian soldiers stormed into Jerusalem and killed countless Turks of all ages. History records that the Crusaders thanked God for their victory whilst wiping their bloodstained swords, standing in pools of blood, inside the Temple of Jerusalem. The genocidal Rwandan Civil War was a re-enactment of the nightmare of the Crusades. Christianity in Rwanda repeated this tragic history that justifies hatred and causes even gentle people to participate in violence and murder.

I also witnessed the exclusivity, aggression, and destruction of religion in Bosnia in 1998. Serbian Eastern Orthodox Christians organized militia groups that burned and slaughtered Bosnian Muslims. The Bosniak women in villages like Grbavica were sexually assaulted in an organized fashion, often by their own Christian neighbors and fellow villagers. How could Christians in their right mind do such things to the women they grew up with in the same villages? Furthermore, in some Muslim societies, when your sister has been raped, even though she is a victim, she may be killed by male family members in a so-called 'honor killing.' Some Muslims also believe that if a Muslim woman who has been raped by a non-Muslim man gives birth to a child, she should be branded an outcast and cursed as an infidel. The perpetrators knew this, and thus their rape was a genocidal program, stealing lives and religion away. Meanwhile, the Serbian Orthodox Christians who committed these mass assaults claimed that they were redeeming these women out of their evil Muslim religion. To take Islam from those Bosniak women is to deprive them of their lives. In the foothills of the Himalayas in Pakistan, children's prayer recitations reverberate breathtakingly across the valleys. When you sail at sunset in Indonesia, The Adzan call-to-prayer from the Mosques echoes over the waves. The sounds of the Mosques always bring me comfort when I'm homesick. For people growing up in an Islamic culture, Islam is life."

That fall, Song returned to Heidelberg. Fortunately, the German Protestant Church Council continued to support his studies. While working on his dissertation, he often looked at the pictures of The Frontiers members posted on the wall of his study, and vowed countless times not to betray their friendship and loyalty. He daily reminded himself of his promise to return to conflict areas to carry out his responsibilities towards Christian peacebuilding, upon completion of his degree. His experience in Africa was incomparably more educational than a mere semester of graduate school and was a great resource during his final oral examination. More importantly, he now knew what it meant, what resolve was needed, and what price one might have to pay, to work for peace in a world of war.

"On the day I defended my dissertation and made it through my oral exams, I knelt down in the exam hall to thank God. Then I headed directly to the Balkan Peninsula, where war clouds were looming. It took 36 hours by bus from Munich, over the Alps, to Bosnia and Herzegovina."

Following the end of the Cold War, many conflicts seemed to take their que from Samuel P. Huntington's idea of fault lines between "civilizations." Peace activists had to predict and prepare for complex conflicts between different cultures, religions and ethnic groups. These conflicts often had a long historical background. Sarajevo was one such place. There were three "civilizations." Catholic and Protestant could be grouped into one, the Eastern Orthodox Church with Russia as its core is the second, and Islam made up the third group. They all met along the borders of Bosnia, Croatia, and Serbia. And Sarajevo was the center of it all.

"On my four-day bus trip along the Balkan Peninsula and around Sarajevo, I saw so many homes destroyed by war it looked like the aftermath of a natural disaster. There were charred-black houses everywhere along the borders, especially in areas that had been culturally diverse. The Christian Serbian soldiers had committed many cruel crimes against their Muslim neighbors. Mostar is a beautiful Bosnian town which had a large, bright, white stone bridge made by the famous Ottoman architect Hayruddin(Hajrudin in Bosnian). The bridge was named Stari Most which means 'old bridge' in Bosnian. It had a half-moon arch, a shape which symbolizes Islam. Under the bridge ran a narrow river. The water under the bridge used to be a playground for all, young and old. To the east of the bridge was a Muslim community and to the west a Catholic one. It was a romantic place where both Catholic and Muslim youth would come to whisper love, and there were many small, historic cafes around it. Basically, the bridge was the cultural center of the whole town.

But when the war broke out, Croatian Catholics blew up the bridge so as to destroy the important Islamic symbol. Before the war, intermarriage between Muslim and Christian was common in Mostar. However, once the war began, many Muslim husbands were executed. Chrysanthemum-patterned scars from grenade explosions still mark the streets. Gates and doors of houses memorialize the dead with photos of missing family. I had been travelling with a young French man from Heidelberg. One day while staying there in Mostar, I fell into a deep sleep and had a dream that I had returned to Korea and my daughter had been missing for days. I was so upset, running the streets looking everywhere for her, I poured my anger and grief out on my parents, screaming that we must sell everything in order to get her back. I tossed and turned in my sleep all night until my companion woke me up, asking me why I had been yelling so much. It was dawn and had just been a nightmare for me. But for many people in Mostar, it was not just a dream but their daily reality. A terrible, hellish reality."

Peace is not perpetual in this world. Those Catholics and Muslims who fell in love with each other and built happy homes in Mostar must have once believed that they would enjoy a lasting peace throughout their lives. But peace is something that require ongoing efforts to maintain and enjoy. In a land where peace is broken, terrible tragedies rage.

"On my way back to Munich from Bosnia and Herzegovina, I

was looking at the snow-covered Balkan Mountains out of the bus windows. I saw old women struggling to cover broken windows with plastic. I saw many newly dug graves and limping children with limbs lost to land mines. However, I could not spot any young adults, not even one. Where on earth could they be? Haupt Strasse in Heidelberg is overflowing with young people, everyone busy enjoying their lives. I thought of the many young people in Korea, probably stuck in libraries working on their exam preparations. I poured my heart into prayer, 'God, please call young people to build peace together in these killing fields, make this a country where justice and peace blossom!' I could already imagine young people coming down over the snow-capped mountains. 'Please, call the youth of the world! Please!' I prayed with tears rolling down."

As he recalls those tears, he begins to weep again.

Chapter 6

Opening Peace School

Song Kang Ho returned to Korea with his Ph.D, but was already searching for another Bosnia. He took note of Indonesia. With its complex mix of ethnic groups and religions as well as its frequent natural disasters, it was a bit like the Balkans of Asia. So only a year after his return from Germany, he headed for East Timor, then one of Indonesia's most troubled regions.

"I returned to Korea in 1998 and left for Indonesia in 1999. Severe conflicts were occurring in Ambon and East Timor. There was religious conflict in Ambon, while in East Timor the mostly Catholic Timorese were fighting for independence from the majority Muslims of Indonesia. The plan was to survey both areas and then open a peace school that I had dreamt of since 1994. However, the situation in East Timor was so dire that I decided to stay there without even visiting Ambon. At that time, increasing international pressure was calling for the Indonesian government to allow East Timor to become independent. During this fight for independence, the suffering and slaughter of the East Timorese people was tremendous. I thought this was a place that really needed peacebuilding and that I wanted to try it here."

East Timor is a small, vulnerable country with a sad history. In 1975, it gained its independence from Portugal after over 400 years of colonization. However, just nine days later, Indonesian forces invaded East Timor and made it an Indonesian province. East Timor claimed its independence once again on May 20, 2002, and finally became a sovereign state in 2002. Song went to East Timor in 1999 in the aftermath of numerous massacres and the prolonged civil unrest that took place during its struggle for independence from Indonesia.

"We arrived in East Timor in September of 1999. The East Timorese had chosen independence from Indonesia through a referendum on August 30th, but pro-Indonesia militias and Indonesian soldiers brutally retaliated for the vote with systematic killings and massacres in places such as Liquiçá, Maliana and Suai. Even some Australian journalists were killed by the Indonesian military, and Australia tried to cover it up, holding closed-door negotiations with Indonesia. Indonesia granted an oil deal to Australia and in return Australia remained silent to Timor-related issues raised by the international community. Meanwhile, Indonesia took an equidistant diplomacy stance towards the US and the former Soviet Union during the Cold War, establishing itself as a sort of political third-party. At the same time, many East Timorese freedom fighters were communists, which Indonesia used to garner western support, labelling the East Timorese, 'Indonesian Cubans.' This granted Indonesia tacit consent for their control over East Timor from the U.S. and much of the international community. The U.K. and other western-aligned world powers sold weapons to Indonesia at that time. East Timor became a Cold War scapegoat and victim of international politics."

Indonesia was brutal to its disputed regions. They mercilessly retaliated against any form of resistance and East Timor was no exception. Song and his team tried to recruit some Indonesians to go into East Timor with them and to witness the wrongdoings committed by their country. The hope was that these Indonesians would return to their county and recruit more people willing to work for peace between East Timor and Indonesia. At the same time, the East Timorese's extreme hatred toward Indonesia would also need to be faced.

"Upon my urging to meet with some local pastors from affected areas, a dozen or so people from around the country gathered at Hosanna Church in Dili, the capital of East Timor. I told them why we were there. I told them that although never easily achieved, reconciliation and peace are one of the most important missions of the Kingdom of God. I encouraged them to invite Indonesian young adults over so that those youths could see the wrongs committed by their nation. I said that those young Indonesians would then return to their country and become peacemakers for both sides. Additionally, I asked them for permission to run a peace camp[2] that would invite young people from all over the world, including Indonesia. After a brief silence, a female pastor named Gomes stood up and prayed aloud, "Lord, I am sorry I can't forgive them yet." She confessed that she was ashamed because although she was a pastor, she was unable to urge for reconciliation. The wound was still so fresh and wide open that even the gentlest of touches was causing her unbearable pain. She had lost all of her family members in the conflict. Another pastor sitting in front of her had also lost more than 10 family members. All the pastors there silently wept. Then Luís, the pastor of Hosanna Church stood up and spoke, "Brother Song, you were not here with us when we were in such agony and fear." His comment struck me hard and filled me with anguish. Those words are still etched in my heart.

We realized that peacebuilding can't just begin once the conflict has ended and everything was safe again. We must be together with them in their agony, when the danger is real. Only then can we earn our right to mediate and build peace. That's why we, The Frontiers, must stand together with those suffering in conflicts, not running away to safety, not evacuating to other countries when danger arises. I used

---

2 Every summer, The Frontiers hold "Peace Camp" programs, inviting young people from around the world to come together in war-stricken areas. The core aim of the program is to open a "Peace School" that encourages the younger generations of war-torn countries to choose reconciliation and coexistence instead of hatred and revenge.

to say to my fellow members of The Frontiers, 'It doesn't matter where you came from before you got here, you're now a Timorese person. At least until you have carried out your mission here, you will share in the communal destiny of the people of East Timor.' This continually caused issues with the Korean Embassy in East Timor. When there was a riot or unrest, they would tell us to quickly leave the country, but we refused. At first, we were a little worried, but as time went by, we knew we had made the right choice. Eventually the Korean embassy staff left the country. When they returned at a safer time, they actually came to us for information on the local situation, as they had lost their field resources."

The distinctive spirit and style of The Frontiers was created and refined in the field in this manner. They responded to and took part in serious conflicts, disasters, and famines around the world. They dashed to conflict zones without delay and tried to live and work like the people there. They sowed the seeds of peace without giving up, and that's how the Peace Camp program started.

"By the end of 1999, we weren't able to bring any Indonesian youth, so we held a sort of partial Peace Camp with international participants numbering nearly eighty young Koreans, and two German youth working for The Frontiers as an alternative to their mandatory military service. We set up a tent and opened Peace School to teach peace to the children. The children seemed bright eyed and peaceful, but when they drew pictures, the boys nearly always drew soldiers and the girls, police. And they would say they wanted to kill the Indonesians who killed their family members. One day as peace school was in session beneath the shade of a tree, some armored vehicles passed by. The children excitedly chased after the convoy. Their eyes lit up when they saw guns, which they admired, expecting these weapons to solve their problems. On the battlefield, gun is god and power comes from the barrel of a gun. For a month, we taught the children stories and songs about peacemakers, as well as general children's songs, and even some Taekwondo. Although we didn't have much water to wash with and all sorts of bugs and insects including fleas and scorpions bit and stung us, it was a valuable experience nurturing the hope for peace."

Peace does not come for free. In *Changing Lenses: A New Focus for Crime and Justice*, Howard Zehr summarizes the concept of "restorative justice," suggesting that instead of punishing certain criminal acts, victims and offenders could go through a common healing process. In other words, the offender seeks forgiveness for the wrongdoing, while actively participating in a guided healing process. Likewise, the victim works through professional guidance to forgive the offender. Zehr argues that through this process, eventually both victim and perpetrator could be restored into co-existent community. East Timor was in dire need of such restorative justice, but it wouldn't be easy, and crisis always loomed during Peace Camp.

"We held our first Peace Forum in Somoxo Village. It was a bit like the South African Truth and Reconciliation Commission. In front of some Indonesian youth we had gathered, we asked the villagers to share their stories of suffering at the hands of Indonesian soldiers. At first there was a solemn silence. People looked at each other and said nothing. Suddenly a villager stood up and spoke angrily to us, 'Who the hell do you think you are? What's the point of bringing all this up again? Why are you twisting the knife in our wounds?' The village chief stepped in to try to calm people down. The chief had been communicating with us. He said to the man, 'Please don't take this the wrong way. They are here to help us reconcile.'

There was a heavy silence. People were very hesitant to bring back their painful memories. After a long silence, a woman finally came forward tell her story. Some Indonesians had set fire to her home, killing her brothers. As she talked, people began to line up behind her to tell their own stories, one by one. After a while, one of the young Indonesians we had brought with us stood up. In tears he said, 'I'm not sure if I can represent our country, but as an Indonesian citizen I am so ashamed and sorry. Please forgive our country.' Of course, it's true, that young man was not the official representative of Indonesia, but in that moment, the atmosphere changed. The villagers called out to him, 'It's not your fault, it was the soldiers! We don't resent you!' The program ran late into the night, with many more people sharing their stories. The East Timorese hugged the Indonesian youths. It was a deeply emotional experience for everyone there.

Thinking that perhaps this is how reconciliation and healing begin, I went outside. The pitch-black sky seemed overwhelmed by starlight, as if the equatorial stars were falling down to earth. The people of Somoxo speak a tribal language called Fatalog and in their language the word for star is 'ipinaka'. A young Korean participant who had followed me outside commented on how beautiful the ipinakas were and that he had no idea that Christianity could be so hands-on and realistic until now, and that he had decided to become a Christian. When did people begin to regard Christianity as a lethargic religion, disconnected from reality? We, Christians, are largely responsible for that. For me, faith in Jesus is the most practical, world-changing, and living faith. Many young people become Christians after joining our peace camps. We don't tell them to go to church. We are not a missionary group. It just happens over time that some of those working with us, see our living faith, and choose the Christian path. Some people find justice and peace through the gospel, and some find the gospel through justice and peace. It's a door that opens from both sides."

Song believes that what is most Christian is also most universal. The true nature of Christianity can be revealed not through so-called Christian language and culture and religious rituals, but through the struggle for justice and peace. These are most common and pressing values for all of humanity. For that very reason, The Frontiers focus their work on justice and peace, not evangelism. Christianity can only bring hope when the gospel is revealed through concrete living.

"The Frontiers[3] grew up in East Timor. We're still learning many things from there. We've learned that for us to be the ambassadors of God's peace in the world, we must be physically present with the people in the most difficult and dangerous times and places of their lives. When people come from all over and put on the loud speaker to "help" once their own safety has been already established, we learned that the local people despise such actions. We also learned from the suffering people that no matter how poor or troubled we

---

3 The Frontiers' Creed
 The Frontiers are Christian radicals and peace builders working to transform violence and injustice in armed conflicts around the world through community-based nonviolence. So as to practice love, righteousness, and peace, The Frontiers attempt to live according to the 10 statements of the following creed:

1. We value justice and peace for humanity more than our own families or national interests.
2. We try to respond to serious conflicts and natural disasters.
3. We are willing to sacrifice our lives for the reconciliation of God.
4. We seek to protect those who are alienated from society, discriminated against, poor, or weak, in accordance with God's will.
5. We will not lie.
6. We seek nonviolence and protest weapons and militarization.
7. We seek to live as servants and we will not inherit nor will any private property.
8. We live in community.
9. We will not swear allegiance to any individual or group, nor support any cause, other than God.
10. We reject unrighteous privileges.

are, we always have the power to love. We found out that in order to truly help someone, you need to help that person to be able to love again."

Part II

"With 'the calmest demeanor' he walked unwaveringly towards truth 'embracing the most convoluted reality.'"

Chapter 7

Gureombi, the Sacred Living Rock

In 2005, Song Kang Ho was in Aceh, located in the northern part of the Indonesian island of Sumatra. A gigantic tsunami had flooded the entire coast of Aceh, wiping out 140,000 people. Countless international groups had entered Aceh to provide aid. However, well before the tsunami disaster, Aceh had already experienced a history of tragedy as a result of long-standing violent conflicts. Motivated by that painful history, The Frontiers went to Aceh to provide emergency relief as well. As they gradually gained trust from the local residents, they began to shift their focus there towards peace building.

"The Frontiers were first dispatched to Aceh in December of 2004, and I joined them the following year to assess the situation. We planned to build a house to live together with children orphaned by the tsunami. So, we began building the house and "Rumoh Meupakat" was chosen as its name. Rumoh Meupakat can mean both 'to decide together' and 'to live together.' It was refreshing that 'deciding together' meant 'living together.' We hoped that the children who grew up in Rumoh Meupakat would eventually be able to work together to help other victims of the Tsunami in even worse conditions. We wanted to encourage those orphan children to be peace builders. Many people in Aceh have suffered from the oppression of the Indonesian central government, and there was hatred in their hearts, but we still wanted to tell the Aceh children about 'living together.'

Following the massive tsunami, the guerrillas feared for their families and villages. Most of the guerilla fighters lived in the mountains fighting for their people and their own families. They longed to return to their homes and see if their loved ones were ok, but couldn't because of all the Indonesian soldiers guarding these villages. Now knowing the news of their families, the guerilla forces' desire to continue their fight gradually faded. Meanwhile, in Helsinki, the representatives of the rebels and Indonesian government were gathered around the negotiating table. Both sides were exhausted from years of war, and in the aftermaths of tsunami it became less clear with whom and for whom they were fighting for. Everyone longed for peace. The Indonesian conservatives strongly opposed it, but with an international committee brokering the peace process, the Acehnese guerrillas began to come down from the mountains to see their families and relatives. They were gone so long that they arrived in chartered buses taking them around the villages for a tour. It was somewhat similar to the family reunion events.[1] A convoy of buses with rebels on them rolling in to tiny rural villages, and huge piles of weapons these guerilla fighters voluntarily returned being cut up and destroyed in local stadiums were symbolic images of people deciding not to wage war or military conflicts any more. It was beautiful. Suddenly, a spring of peace had come to Aceh."

God's love can sometimes seem desperate. God loves us so much that he wants to save us at the expense of destroying everything. In a land of despair, where everything had collapsed, God began a peace mission. Aceh was completely devasted by the tremendous tsunami, yet with that tsunami came the cautious beginnings of peace and reconciliation in the land. If we really put our hope in God, we cannot be discouraged by anything, including despair.

It was around this time, while Song was in Aceh, that he heard the news that Jeju Island would be designated as the "Island of World Peace" Hope filled his heart at the thought that Korea might one day become a nation without war.

In 1990, then leader of the Soviet Union, Mikhail Gorbachev, made a surprise visit to Jeju Island. It was a harbinger of the end

---

[1] Note to English readers: During the Korean War, millions of families were separated and many of them never heard from their missing members again. In 1983, 30 years after the end of war, Korean Broadcasting System (KBS) aired a series of missing family member ads and successfully reunited thousands of families live on TV. This led to a series of family reunion events in South Korea as well as reunion events for families separated by the North and South Korean border.

of Cold War era, and a significant historical event for Korea. In June the following year, a paper titled, "The Northeast Asian Order and "Jeju Island: A Proposal for the Island of Peace" was published at a conference commemorating the founding of the Jeju Global Society. In 2001, Korean domestic and international scholars began gathering regularly to hold the Jeju Peace Forum at the newly established Jeju International Peace Center. Finally, in 2005, Jeju was officially designated the "Island of World Peace." This designation made sense because Jeju Island is situated at the geopolitical center of Northeast Asia. But additionally, Jeju Island is a land of great tragedy, with the desperate need for peace. The scars of the 4.3 Uprising, one of the most heart-wrenching events in Korean history, have not yet fully healed. Jeju islanders are still not fully comfortable with mainland Koreans, and many are still unable to speak about the incident. On April 3rd of each year, nearly every household in these villages will hold a memorial ritual for a family member lost during the 4.3 Uprising. Such painstaking memories of extreme suffering and sorrow ironically also serves as a testimony for the need of peace in Jeju Island.

"I had long thought, 'I must visit Jeju Island. It might just be the land of hope I've been looking for.' Even in Aceh, Jeju always had a place in the back of my head. When I finally made it to Jeju in the spring of 2006, the first place I visited was the 4.3 Peace Memorial. Although the national government had officially apologized by that time, the 4.3 Uprising remains an unhealed wound for many Jeju islanders. As I walked through the memorial hall, I developed a strong attachment to the history of Jeju. The following year, in 2007, I was able to visit Gangjeong for the first time, but as I was still heavily involved with work in other countries, my visits to Jeju were only brief.

Gangjeong used to be a peaceful village where farmers grew tangerine trees and old haenyeo[2] divers tended to the sea. Then, in 2007, the Korean government abruptly announced that it would build a large naval base and seaport across the Gangjeong coast. When I visited in 2007, the atmosphere was quite different from what you see now. Back then, several hundred villagers used to gather to protest, and flags opposing the naval base were displayed everywhere. Residents greeted me politely, but the atmosphere was sort of, 'Why did this guy come, and what can he really do?' Part of it was that they didn't really trust the 'mainland people' (non-islanders from the Korean peninsula) like me, and part of it was confidence in their presumed victory. Their cause was just, and so many villagers were strongly opposed to the project. They thought they would definitely win. So, I was just sort of a visiting guest."

---

2 Note to English readers: Haenyeo, literally meaning "sea women" in Korean, refer to Jeju's professional free diving female sea harvesters. Women divers in Jeju are a tradition that dates back to at least the 17th century. By the 18th century, female divers outnumbered male counterparts and eventually, nearly all divers in Jeju were women, many of them often being the sole breadwinners of their families. Haenyeo harvests remained a prominent percentage of Jeju's fishery revenue for many years, but the number of haenyeos have slowly declined with most of the remaining haenyeo now being elderly women.

The Gangjeong villagers were too naive. Their optimism was understandable, but it wasn't long before it began to crumble. Their opponent was cunning, calculating, and above all, in control. It was too much for the villagers.

"The navy hurriedly dealt with the naval base proposal and its surrounding issues, issues that affected the future of a village and the interests of an entire population, in just a few days. There was not a single briefing or public hearing on the naval base construction project. The navy privately offered 100 million KRW each to a group of haenyeo divers on the condition that they give up diving in the coast off Gangjeong. They then secretly bribed a few of the other villagers to outwardly support the construction plans, in an attempt to show that the base construction was popular and desired. Next, before most villagers were even aware of the naval base project, they hastily called an irregular village meeting with no advance notice, which only eighty-seven residents attended, mostly those previously contacted by the navy. The meeting involved multiple procedural violations and the vote to approve the naval base project was done via clapping. When the rest of the villagers learned what had happened, they quickly impeached the village mayor who had pushed for and manipulated the irregular meeting, elected a new mayor, and held a proper general village meeting. This time sixty-nine percent of the population voted with ninety-four percent voting against the naval base project. Nevertheless, the navy ignored the vote, and pushed ahead with their unilateral plan as if conducting some kind of military operation.

Soon the community began to crumble. The residents of Gangjeong Village, who have been like family for generations, were now divided between those in favor and those against the base construction. The division, conflict, and arguments became so fierce that the two sides became each other's worst enemies. People wouldn't even go to each other's weddings and funerals anymore. Parents were divided from their children, and siblings cut each other out. When you walk around the village, you will see yellow flags with the words 'Absolutely Opposed to the Naval Base' in black letters, put up by those against the base. Those in favor of the base put up Korean national flag atop tall bamboo poles. You would feel like walking through a battlefield.

The military is supposed to prevent war and preserve peace, but on the contrary, it was deliberately causing more conflict and division. And it's the Gangjeong residents that have to suffer. The navy will stop at nothing to build this base. They are completely indifferent to this conflict they've created, to the annihilation of this community, and to the destruction of this natural environment. Gangjeong coast is an exceptional ecological treasure. Cultural Heritage Administration designated several species and places in this area as natural monuments, and Gangjeong coast is also the home to several endangered plants and animals. But the military wants to pour concrete over all of it and fill the area with warships, nuclear submarines, and aircraft carriers.

Things started to get even worse for the villagers in 2009. There were several reasons why, but the biggest was losing a lawsuit that they thought they were going to win for sure. The villagers had filed a lawsuit entitled, 'Confirmation of Invalidation on the Approval of Defense and Military Facility Project Implementation Plan,' over the navy's failure to conduct an environmental impact assessment (EIA). The lawsuit was a lengthy ordeal and during the trial, the navy hurriedly conducted a quick EIA. To the villagers' shock, the court ruled that while they recognize the fact that the navy had indeed failed to conduct a proper EIA before moving forward with construction plans, the court still considers the EIA conducted during the trial to be valid. In the meanwhile, despite everything that was going on, the navy requested the Jeju Governor to remove Gangjeong's 'Absolute Preservation Area' status, and the Jeju Provincial Assembly hastily passed this removal without proper hearings. In turn the villagers filed yet another lawsuit, 'Suspension and Invalidation of the Absolute Preservation Area Change Disposition.' In 2010, the Jeju District Court dismissed their lawsuit, claiming that the villagers were not qualified to be the plaintiffs of such a lawsuit. It was clear as the light of day that the courts were clearly on the side of the navy. Towards the end of 2010, the 2011 National Assembly budget that included funding for the base construction was passed, again without proper hearings. The villagers rapidly began to lose their momentum as judicial avenues to fight the injustice dried up. During the gubernatorial elections that year, disagreements and divisions between the anti-naval base villagers begin to emerge. At that time there weren't any outside activists to help keep the movement going."

Another issue among residents opposing the naval base was an internal debate over what constituted a peaceful protest. Some villagers believed that only protests within legal bounds were legitimately peaceful, while others argued that protests could go beyond legal boundaries without being classified as violent. This debate effectively split the protesting villagers, creating a moderate group insisting on only using legal methods to protest, and a more radical group willing to use illegal tactics as long as they were non-violent. This new internal division worsened when provincial politicians took advantage of the moderate opposition group during the 2010 election for Jeju governor. Eventually, as the naval base construction become official, the moderate group was persuaded to join the more radical group, but the movement was slowly falling apart. Song found this tremendously heartbreaking.

"In January of 2011, I stayed in 'Joongdeoksa Temple,' the nickname for a makeshift greenhouse on Gureombi were a man named Yang Yoon Mo was living. For a week, I tried to imagine what I could do for Gangjeong. Unlike my previous visit to Gangjeong, the village atmosphere was depressed. While I stayed at Joongdeoksa Temple, two villagers, Kim Jong Hwan and Goh Jong In, brought me a heater and would visit me nightly to see if I was warm enough and take care of me in many ways. Jong Hwan would drink makgeolli(rice wine) and lament the loss of momentum in the village. He would cook me ramen or stew every night. After a week on Jeju Island, I returned to the mainland to The Frontiers' community near Yangpyeong. But Jong Hwan's lament still rang in my ears, his voice like the sigh of man on his knees, bound and gagged, about to be devoured by a beast.

The Kingdom of God is a kingdom of justice and peace, and anyone who seeks God's Kingdom and its righteousness should pray for justice to overcome injustice in the land. Even if you don't have the strength to fight, you can still pray. Isn't it a Christian's work to pray for peace and reconciliation in a village divided in two, so torn apart that family members and former friends won't attend each other's funerals or weddings, where a nephew will threaten to kill his own uncle? I couldn't find hope that the villagers would rise again to fight and win. But I thought, I'll at least go to a part of Gureombi where no one comes and pray for God's Kingdom of justice to come. There is a flat, stage-like spot on Gureombi and when I saw it at dawn, I immediately felt the need to kneel down and pray in that empty space. Usually, when members of The Frontiers pray together, we do so in silence, but there, where no one could hear me, I naturally felt compelled to pray loudly, crying out to God as if for the first time."

Chapter 8

God's Calling

"I wanted to go back to Gangjeong as soon as I could, but various things kept delaying me. One day I received an invitation from general office of SPARK(Solidarity for Peace and Reunification in Korea)3. I didn't know anyone who worked for SPARK. Of course, they are known for their storied work and activism, but I had never joined any of their activities and didn't know much about them. Out of curiosity, I decided to accept the invitation and see what kind of organization they were, and when I got there, I ran into Yang Yoon Mo again. I thought happily, 'Wow, that's the guy I stayed with at Joongdeoksa Temple in Gangjeong!' But he seemed desperate and implored me, 'Hurry and come back to Gangjeong!' His distressed

---

3 SPARK(Solidarity for Peace and Reunification in Korea) is an organization formed in 1994 by a coalition of some of Korea's first peace groups and activists from the Anti-Nuclear Peace Movement Alliance, New Peace Movement Peoples Group, and the Solidarity Council for Peace and Unity. SPARK works towards peace, disarmament, and reunification of the Korean peninsula.

appeal shook my conscience. This was mid-February. I immediately decided to drop what I was working on and return to Gangjeong as soon as possible. Soon several other members of The Frontiers and I were back defending Joongdeoksa Temple and the villagers were happy to welcome us, saying our return gave them new hope to fight again when all seemed lost."

Yang Yoon Mo is a film director and critic from Jeju Island, and he was one of main reasons why Song stayed to fight for Gangjeong. Yang was first arrested in April of 2011 while protesting the naval base. While staying in Jeju Prison he went on a seventy-one-day hunger strike. When he was arrested again the following year, he went on a forty-two-day hunger strike. For three years before his arrest, he had lived in the Joongdeoksa Temple greenhouse tent he had pitched. Gureombi had become a part of him. Yang was yet another 'significant encounter' for Song.

"When someone's story deeply touches my heart, I often regard it as a call from God, thinking, 'Isn't God trying to say something to me through this person?' That day Yang Yoon Mo's desperate appeal came as a rebuke to me, 'Why are you delaying what you must do, what you've already decided to do so?' I had many excuses, but I decided to take care of my own affairs as soon as possible and go. I had a feeling that there might be a long road ahead, but eventually I put everything behind me and went back to Gangjeong. And it's already been a year now.

At that time, the depressed atmosphere of the village made it difficult to think about how to keep fighting. But I came to Gangjeong to pray, so my main work was just to eat and pray on Gureombi. At first, I tried to pray three times a day: morning, lunch and dinner, but there were always people around at lunch and I felt awkward kneeling to pray on the rock, so I decided to just pray in the morning and at sunset. Thus, I had a lot of free time during the day. Since I had come with some co-workers, we rented a house nearby for three months. Typically, in our organization, we plan to carry out work for at least a year at a time, but since we didn't really know how things would happen in Gangjeong, we just made a three-month contract. So, we fixed up that house a bit, but later found this house we live in now, and moved here at the recommendation of some villagers. At first, most villagers did not particularly welcome our presence, but after a month or so they began to slowly open their hearts to us. They seemed to appreciate our intention to stay with them long-term in their fight for justice.

Yang Yoon Mo came back to the village around mid-March. From April 6th of that year, the actual base construction started. One day, Yang chucked a rock at the construction vehicle of an employee from the Busan-based subcontractor. By sheer chance, it somehow went through the open window and hit the driver of a running car. Subsequently, Yang was arrested. If I hadn't known him well, I might have thought he was violent, but he's not that kind of person. When he's at the naval base construction site discussing the issue, he's a very logical and gentle person. I once saw him lay down face first on Gureombi with arms outstretched saying it felt like a mother's embrace. He is person who truly loves Gureombi. He had been the president of the Korean Film Critics Association, living on the Korean mainland, but he returned to his home of Jeju and protecting the environment and Gureombi became his new way of life. He loved nature so much, sometimes he could turn into a beast to protect it. He was back protesting and this time he was assaulted and violently arrested by the police. Fortunately, some young people from a group called 'Christian Youth Academy' were visiting that day and managed to record video of the situation with their phones, some of them even live streaming. The videos of his assault spread online and went viral on Twitter.

That night after his arrest, in his now empty Joongdeoksa Temple, I thought to myself, 'Okay older brother, I will defend what you were trying to protect until you return.' I prayed for him every day and he soon started his first prison hunger strike. Through his willingness to put his own life in danger, I could feel his sincerity. It was not just bravery but desperation that drove him to act. So, I decided, 'I will protect Joongdeoksa Temple while my brother is away. I will do the work that he did in his place until he returns.' Until then I had only prayed in Gangjeong, but from then on, I began to take action."

Indeed, Song Kang Ho was transformed into a fighter. He had

simply planned to take Yang's place for a time, but his protest actions were even more wild. He stopped and occupied an excavator. He jumped into an area where cement was being poured. In order to block heavy equipment from the Samsung and Daelim construction companies, he hung a chain from a quickly erectly metal tent frame and wrapped it around his neck as Anglican Fr. Kim Kyung Il held his legs. In such extreme situations, Song would remain calm, sometimes even cheerful. That day the construction company workers eventually gave up and withdrew. Some people were delighted by this small victory, but others were shocked by his actions. Some colleagues and village residents were worried for his safety. He asked himself, "Are you really prepared to die to stop the naval base? Are you really that determined of a person?"

> "In dramatic and extreme situations, I try to ask myself simple questions with simple answers. I did this that day when that huge heavy equipment was coming, and I tried to block it with a chain around my neck. I thought, if a naval base is built here and leads to another war, but my sacrifice could lead to a greater resistance and block that path to war, I can save the many lives that would have been sacrificed in that war. So why shouldn't I die for this? How can it a be a waste to give my life for such a meaningful and valuable cause when so many people just die on the street in traffic accidents or on hospital beds? The answer was clear to me. 'I'm willing to give my life to stop war. You can blow me up, you can drown me in cement. That's

where I'll die if I must!'"

To use the words of the poet, Park Noh Hae, Song walked towards the truth "with the calmest deamor while embracing the most convoluted reality."

> We are now devoting our time, materials, and most sincere efforts to the kingdom of God. And we also wait for that decisive moment when we finally can give our own lives. It is only in this waiting that I realized what it meant that the first church members expected and prayed for martyrdom. So, Let's wait in anticipation of drinking from that cup of fate that even Jesus could not avoid. Then, when that day comes, let's live brilliantly in our final moments as witnesses of Christ, with praise for the magnificence of life and gratitude to all those who loved us. Let's hope that our deaths may be the culmination of our lives. We're already dead anyway, our lives but a gift of grace. How we live is important but so too is how we die. Let's prepare for a death without regret.
>
> - "The Frontiers Monthly Magazine," February 2005

For a time, Song managed to block the navy's influence in the village, but he believed that all the villagers needed be on the same path to fight against the power of the navy that had separated and divided them. Regardless of any advantages or disadvantages of the naval base project, it was up to the villagers as a collective community to come together to determine their fate. Only then could reconciliation and peace amongst all the people of Gangjeong be achieved. As for himself, the struggle to stop the naval base was now his inevitable destiny.

> "I prayed for wisdom and courage every morning on Gureombi rock. If we can't cut off this evil that continues to flow into the village, and end this spirit of unjust and illegal division, the villagers will not find peace and reconciliation. When I first came here, I hoped that I would play the role of a mediator for peace and reconciliation, but this was a naive, formalistic and unfeasible hope. The navy holds too much power. The energy of conflict and division springs from the naval base project, and it must be stopped. If we fail to fundamentally root it out, Gangjeong will never again be whole as a community."

God is with those who suffer in a land of injustice and violence. God wills us to dream of justice and peace in such a land. Song won the hearts of the Gangjeong residents and became their trusted friend. But he is not alone. Many people opposing the base have flocked to Gangjeong, many of them staying long-term to fight and now living as residents of the village.

Chapter 9

Naval Base and the Island of Peace

In Korea, there were some people who supported the opposition to the naval base construction project but at the same time criticized those who engaged in tactics that broke the law. They questioned why someone who came to make peace would ignore the law. There were also those that demanded all "outside" activists to leave Gangjeong. However, the real "outside" forces are those who would build a naval base on Jeju, the Island of Peace. The world-renowned scholar, MIT Professor Noam Chomsky, sent this message of solidarity to the imprisoned, hunger-striking Yang Yoon Mo:

> "I would like to express my deepest respect for those who are resisting the ongoing destruction on Jeju Island caused by the naval base construction. It will only lead to the worsening of military competition. Jeju Island is an island of peace and should always be. Above

all, I pay special homage to the courage and commitment of Mr. Yang Yoon Mo, who is in prison at the moment, undertaking a hunger strike against the destructive policies that will result in disaster for the people of Korea, their neighboring countries, and eventually the whole world."

In the above statement, Professor Chomsky is primarily concerned with the heightened risk of conflict in the region that the construction of a new naval base would bring. In a separate interview, he stressed the importance of efforts to preserve Jeju's beautiful UNESCO World Heritage-listed environment, while also expressing concern that the construction of a military base would increase international military tensions and the threat of war, even nuclear war. For Chomsky, the key purpose for the construction of the Jeju Naval base is for the U.S., which maintains hegemonic control over much of Pacific region, to hold China in check.4 Song maintains a similar opinion on the matter.

"War is a terrible thing. No matter how hard our struggles get now, it's still easier than war. When people here are afraid, I ask them what they are afraid of. Those we are fighting against now generally follow some sort of bare minimum regulations. They aren't actively trying to kill you. This fight is doable because it is not a battle to the death. They might throw you in prison, but prison is not always so

---

4 See http://youtu.be/5laCn5I5Ey4

bad. Of course, imprisonment is unpleasant, but prison can teach you things as well. And messages from prison always have a strong appeal to those on the outside. Being in prison is just a sacrifice for the cause. Considering all this, this fight is worth trying.

Most conflict areas are in a state of war. It's difficult to access these places and relief work there is difficult. The risk is extremely high. Of course, there is work to be done in such places and it's important that peace activists be willing to do that work, but the work can sometimes be limited in certain ways. The Frontiers have mostly been active in areas where a precarious peace has just begun to form, post-war. East Timor and Aceh were mostly in post-conflict conditions. Jeju, on the other hand, is currently in a kind of pre-conflict condition, which could eventually lead to the outbreak of war. There are still many opportunities for us to intervene. We need to engage in practical pre-emptive action to neutralize the threat of war at this stage, rather than waiting for the outbreak of war before we respond. If the naval base construction project is suspended there might be some unexpected repercussions, but whatever they are, they will be incomparable to the repercussions of a war."

The Korean government and naval authorities claim that the construction of the naval base is in prevention of war. However, as Chomsky suspects, China is likely to view the construction as part of U.S. military strategy against them. Why, then, would the Korean government push ahead in this irrational manner? Wouldn't making Jeju Island a peaceful buffer zone and therefore an actual "Island of Peace" be a more effective strategy to promote international peace? Song suspected that other insidious interests lay behind the Korean government's decisions and actions.

> "The government just slapped the title 'Island of Peace' on Jeju without actually doing much else. But the government has actively protected the commercial interests and capital of chaebol(mega-corporations) under the title of "defense industry." Money and the sword go hand-in-hand with capitalism. Swords protect money, and money make swords. I believe the two pillars that constrain us and uphold modern society are money and swords, the chaebol and the warlords."

Christians, called to be peacemakers, were impotent on Jeju Island. Most of the churches on Jeju were either in favor of the naval base construction or "impartially" uninterested. Some of the more extremist conservative churches even criticized other Christians who were against the Gangjeong Naval Base.

> "The ideologies of material prosperity and national security are very much in control. The government, the military, and the giant chaebol corporations collude with each to protect and justify their mutual interests. And the church is no different. During our country's process of economic growth, many mainstream churches colluded with power,

gaining economic favors from the state in return. They grew rapidly, but serving their own twisted ideologies. We've traded our most basic faith in service of Yahweh God for the god of security. These churches teach their members that the state is essential to the church and its faith, but this is neither biblical nor historical. Many churches have the logic of the national security deeply rooted in their ideologies. Thus, economic values often supersede faith values. They have laid down the fundamental mission and values of the church and painted a Christian veneer on the ideology of the world. The church itself is now thoroughly secularized, repackaging the values of the world as Christianity.

The core values of Christianity are not violence and material goods, but the life and freedom found through justice, peace, and joy. That's why the designation of Jeju Island as the 'Island of World Peace' should be so significant. But now the government wants to build a military base here. As the Korean peninsula is situated in the physical center of Northeast Asian geopolitics, it has long served as a base for militaries through wars, cold wars, conflicts and political disputes. Korea has seen enough tragedy. Jeju Island should now become a true peace island that symbolizes and creates peace between the nations."

Song longs for Jeju to become a demilitarized island of peace. He argues that not only should the naval base construction be immediately ceased, but that all existing marine and air bases and forces should be withdrawn from the island.

"Alddreu Airfield in Moseulpo, Jeju, used to be an imperial Japanese airfield but now is under the jurisdiction of the Korea Ministry of National Defense. It is my hope that both it and Gureombi can be transformed into public peace parks where people can come to sing, dance, learn. Places that encourage the spread of peace throughout the world. I don't want Jeju to once again become an 'unsinkable aircraft carrier,'[5] with airfields and naval bases filled with bombers, warships and nuclear submarines equipped with devastating weapons. I hope that in the future Jeju Island is a completely demilitarized peace island without bases and soldiers. I hope this island will become a tugboat that will lead all of Korea to becoming a demilitarized, peaceful, and neutral nation. Our mission of these times is to push forward peace in Northeast Asia both with and between China, Japan, Russia, and the U.S."

---

5 Looking ahead to war with China during its colonial occupation of Korea, Japan referred to Jeju Island as an "unsinkable aircraft carrier."

Chapter 10

He Is Just Where He Should Be Right Now

Gangjeong village has a church. With around 250 of Gangjeong's 1,900 residents attending, it was a sizable church for such a small town. It also had a good reputation among villagers for transforming lives. An alcoholic attendee had overcome his addiction, an abusive husband was reformed. Yet, the church was impotent in the face of the giant wave that was the naval base construction. The church preached peace yet took no action towards fostering peacemakers. Nor did it know how to work to build peace in the broader community. The church had forsaken justice and conformed to the ideology of security and prosperity. When the village mayor was locked up in jail for three months, the church did not visit or comfort him. Eventually that church could not help but suffer the pain of division, torn apart by the naval base project.

"In some ways, Gangjeong church is a microcosm, a quintessentially typical Korean church. At first glance, the Korean church seems mature and genuine in its faith. Yet, they seldom speak up against the many injustices in Korean society such as those caused by redevelopment. Most churches did nothing and just sat by as spectators during the Yongsan Namildang demolition and eviction disaster. The head of the redevelopment association and some of the tenants who were killed in the fire while protesting their eviction were not only Christians but members of the same church! Christians in Rwanda were supposedly 90% of the population at the time of the genocide. It didn't matter. 25% of Koreans are Christian? It's all in vain. The Christianity spread in Africa was the Christianity of the empire, a diseased Christianity. It was as if someone needing blood got a blood transfusion from an AIDS patient. Maybe you can prolong your life right away, but eventually you will die, little by little, from the disease.

The barometer for healthy Christianity is the following questions: 'Is the church talking about Justice? Does the church practice peace?' If a church can't answer these questions in earnest and with its actions, that is an unhealthy Christianity. That's like churches during colonial era that were unable to fully preach on the book of Exodus. It's not just the Korean church. Indonesia, as a former Dutch colony, is like this too, and Africa's the same way. A Christianity that does not genuinely proclaim the truth and put it into practice is like a house built on sand. When conflict comes it will not last long. The difference between a house built on stone and a house built on sand is whether what is proclaimed is put into practice. What you do is what you actually believe. Indonesian pastors remained silent when their government ruthlessly oppressed East Timor. During the East Timor's independence process, Indonesian pastors even acted as informants to the police, identifying and supplying information about East Timorese pastors who helped and supported the independence movement. As a result, all Indonesian churches in East Timor were burned down. If you visit Suai or Maliana, you can see the ruins of destroyed and burned down churches. Some of them are empty, others are used for livestock. This kind of thing is not just an old story, it still goes on. In his book Peace Child, Don Richardson tells the story of a group of passionate missionaries in the occupied Papua province of Indonesia. However, there was no teaching of justice in the message spread by those missionaries as the oppressive Indonesian government put pressure on missionaries and pastors who tried to speak of justice. Now Papua has more Christians that any other region, but for what? Those countless churches of Papua are built on the foundation of sand."

Song is not only here because of Gangjeong village or Gureombi rock. It is ultimately for the Kingdom of God that he chains himself, jumps into the sea, is beaten, insulted, thrown in prison, and risks his life. For Song, justice and peace are the true symbols of the Kingdom of God. Thus, he cannot simply just leave a place where justice is broken, and peace has collapsed. He might be beaten, wounded, bruised, or detained, but he can't just back away. When the hope of peace fades, he finds reason to remain. He is just where he should be right now.

> "It is not only Christians who do God's work. Those who say, 'Since we are doing God's work, let's work among Christians,' are those that still don't know what God's work is. We need to be able to see that God's work is beyond prejudice. Institutionalized churches, churches in collusion with power, churches silent to injustice; these churches don't lead us on the path of God. Justice and peace are the values that will light the way. Reading the bible and prayer can be valuable tools, but not just for the sake of doing them. Done for their own sake, they are not really worth doing. Their purpose is to aid us in establishing the Kingdom of God, where justice and peace are practiced and preserved, in this land of despair.

> In Gangjeong, I became a criminal and was imprisoned for the first time. Here, if I live according to what I think is right, I will become the enemy of the Korean government. Sometimes people criticize me, 'Why are you meddling there, what are you doing?' But I have no doubts. I truly believe that what I'm doing here is my work and the right thing to do, no matter the price I might pay. In Korea, this kind of struggle is all over the country, not just here in Gangjeong. These are the kinds of the places that Christians should flock, but instead churches seem to trap them in their sanctuary fortresses. Watching the enthusiasm of young people at big church worship ser-

vices and missionary group gatherings, I once had expectations like, 'How great would it be if these youth came to a site like Gangjeong, and we worked and sweated together.' But while those mission programs gather crowds of young people, relatively few people visit Gangjeong. In fact, many young Christians study at a missionary training center just a short distance from Gangjeong, vowing to be witnesses to Christ and the gospel to the 'ends of the earth,' but only a few make it to Gangjeong, the 'end of the earth' right next door. It truly disappoints me."

Although he spoke of immense frustration, the look on Song's face remained calm. It was the same look he had when he told me about this vision for peace school in the African refugee camp. Perhaps he sees the same vision here in Gangjeong and is dreaming of a new dawn, when the youth of Korea take up the cause of justice in Gangjeong and everywhere it is called for. Thinking back, Song was often smiling, yet with tears in his eyes. Is it sadness? Is it something he is envisioning? My interview time was almost up, and I asked, "What else are you dreaming of?"

"There are two things I want to do in the future. First, I want to return to my hometown. Even now, when I hear news of blood running in the streets of democracy struggles in the Middle East and the civil war in Syria, I feel a burden of debt. My hometown is there, where there is suffering. Even as I work in Gangjeong, I feel a kind of guilt about the painful reality that they suffer from.

Nevertheless, I think that another important task lies before me in the future, for the peace of our nation, and it may be my final ministry. In one word, reunification. I'm not going to comment on how I hope to accomplish that now since it is somewhat radical and dangerous, but I've always been a simple person. I have always believed that meeting face-to-face was the most efficient way. We'll have to get around the South Korean National Security Act and its North Korean counterpart, but we are one people. There is no faster path than the experience of meeting each other face-to-face. So even when I was stuck in prison, I thought, 'Might as well experience now what I'll have to experience later anyway.'

Unfortunately, the reality is that being a Christian and living for peace will many times lead to punishment and imprisonment under the laws of this world. In the past, I thought I might be able to avoid that, but that was very naive. Society does not tolerate the essential values of the Kingdom of God. Power is always selfish, and society runs on collective selfishness, pursuing private interests rather than truth. Therefore, those who want to realize the values of truth, justice, freedom, life, and peace must act beyond the laws of the state. That's why we see that Jesus's disciples couldn't help but spend time in prison. It's very clear to me. Gangjeong is the same. If I am to work here as a Christian, it was inevitable that I would be ensnared by the law. If you don't want to go to prison, you have to stay away from places like Gangjeong. Only then could a Christian live without being punished by the law.

But most importantly, God calls us to places like Gangjeong where justice has been crushed beneath injustice, and peace repressed by violence. People of these places are being wronged and they cry out in suffering. God is already there with them in their anguish. We must be able to hear God's heartbeat, God's deep sighs in a place like this. That's why Gangjeong is a precious and sacred place. In my own pedagogical expression, Gangjeong is 'God's school.' Those that ask why we must go to conflict areas like Gangjeong, Kurdistan, Afghanistan, or Iraq miss the point. God's heart calls us to be God's hands and feet, to embrace, to comfort, and to care. Christians must go to such places of pain and sorrow, because God seeks people to go to such places. It is in these types of places that we can see true human change, because it is where you experience God. Therefore, if churches and mission organizations were to send young people to a place like Gangjeong, not only would those young people be able to bring comfort to suffering people, but also, they themselves will grow in maturity. The places where God resides with his people are these places where death and life intersect, where there is desperate pain and unbearable suffering, where we might refer to as 'hellish' places. That's why I tell young people to not search for heaven, but for hell. At least in this world."

Song is a very dangerous person. But maybe that's how Christian life should be. Just a few days after our interview, on April 1st, the Palm Sunday marking the beginning of the Holy Week,

Song was arrested. It also happened to be his fifty-fifth birthday. On April 3rd, Jeju's historic day of sadness, Song Kang Ho was imprisoned.

Part III

"*Like a flock of geese flying in formation, the villagers and peacekeepers of Gangjeong are united together in our search for that far-off land of peace.*"

Chapter 11

God's Hope Begins When We Become Hopeless

Song Kang Ho was arrested for the first time on July 17, 2011, on the charge of Obstruction of Business and was released on probation 11 days later, on July 28. He has engaged in peace work in many conflict areas, but this was his first arrest. He submitted an appeal regarding the appropriateness of his arrest warrant as follows:

Your Honor,

I have lived my life of fifty years opposing war and working to making peace. To that end, I have travelled around the world to various conflict zones such as Rwanda, Bosnia, Somalia, East Timor, Afghanistan, and Kashmir. I have struggled with the terror of war, witnessing the tears and suffering of its victims. The reason I am opposed to construction of a naval base in Gangjeong Village in Jeju is that I have experienced the devastation of war and its horrors to a great degree. The government and navy are claiming that the construction's purpose is development of resources near the underwater reef of Ieodo Island, and to secure southern shipping routes, but I think they are just a pretext and do not demonstrate the deeper motive. Even if what the government and navy claim are indeed the real motivation behind this construction, I believe the consequent militaristic attempt for a power game against China and Japan is not only unrealistic but dangerous.

I also cannot shake the suspicion that the fundamental reasoning behind building this naval base, and thereby destroying the beautiful nature of Gangjeong village, is not countering some grave national military threat, but a greedy nepotistic project designed to fill certain pockets. It is out of pure greed that the land of one of the safest, most beautiful, and most peaceful small villages has been taken by force, that this Absolute Conservation Area has been stolen and will be covered with the concrete of a naval base ever-so increasing the risk of war.

Sometimes, I have attempted to look at this from the navy's perspective, to see if perhaps the anti-base movement is wrong. At the entrance to the naval base construction site, there is a billboard depicting the finished base. Wouldn't such a large and fancy base develop the village of Gangjeong? I've considered this aspect. However, if you sit on Gureombi rock on the Joongdoek coast and just take a look around, you will soon wake up from the fantastical illusion of that billboard.

From behind, Mt. Halla's elegant and magnificent figure surrounds you, and to the front, Beom Island, Mun Island, and Seop Island float on the sea like traditional oriental paintings. Clean fresh water shoots up from the springs of Gureombi Rock, a rock formation so intricately created that no human effort would be able to mimic it. Anyone with a heart has no choice but to instinctively refuse to cover this living, breathing rock with cement or an artificial structure. It goes without saying that building this naval base will destroy all this natural beauty. Not only is the plan for a naval base in Gangjeong already increasing tension in the Northeast Asian region, the implementation process has been full of problematic issues.

First, this project disregards the democratic processes that are the foundation of our society. Yes, the village meeting held on April 26, 2007 was a complete hoax, conducted without proper notice, and the proposal passed with the pre-bought votes. They say they conducted a telephone survey in May of 2007, yet they won't disclose the contents of the survey, nor allow the results to be audited. It seems the only reason for the existence of this survey was to achieve navy's own goals. How can you handle such a significant matter with such haste, when that matter will determine the fate of an entire community for generations? If the navy and the government had sufficiently gathered the residents' opinions and followed due process, the villagers would not have spent five years, and many of their livelihoods, to fight against the Jeju Naval Base Construction Project. The navy claims to have already spent 100 billion KRW on construction costs for the project and thus it's too late to back down. But for the purpose of upholding the democratic principles that are the basis of our constitution and the foundation of our society, 100 billion KRW or even 1 trillion KRW can't be considered a loss.

Second, a naval base on the "Island of Peace" would harm, not increase, the country's national security. The navy claims that national security can only be safeguarded by military violence. However, the clear purpose for the Jeju Naval Base is not to counteract some North Korean invasion, but to keep China and Japan in check. The navy already has the 2nd Fleet stationed to the west at Pyeongtaek to watch China, and the 3rd Fleet to the south at Busan to keep Japan in check. Meanwhile, the largest group of tourists to Jeju are Chinese tourists, followed by Japanese tourists. It is not a place to prepare to fight against China and Japan but a place to make political and diplomatic efforts to develop stronger and friendlier relations with them. The idea of increasing our military power to keep China in check would be just as unrealistic and dangerous as trying to increase our military power to keep the U.S. in check. This will inevitably lead to devastating consequences that would truly and seriously threaten our national security in the future. The Jeju Naval Base is an idea that stems from arrogant militarism. Maritime security, counter to what the navy claims, is the duty of the coast guard, not the navy. The possibility of border disputes near Ieodo Island should be handled politically and diplomatically. If we try to solve such problems militarily, our country could suffer greatly from the catastrophe that is war.

Under the US-ROK Mutual Defense Treaty, a naval base built on Jeju Island will also encourage U.S. imperial military ambitions and will be used by the U.S. military to contain China. It will be just a matter of time before this naval base drags Korea into a war between China and the U.S. over the hegemony in Northeast Asia. Once again, we will become a victim of tragic history. Jeju Island should learn the lessons of its history, hear the wishes of the victims of the 4.3 Uprising, and become a demilitarized island of peace. Remember that the 4.3 Uprising followed Japanese militarism and its resulting military fortification of Jeju Island. Military fortifications invite war and war leads to mass death on the surrounding lands. Before the blood of the original 4.3 Uprising has fully dried, we are following another reckless course towards a tragic future. Remember that Hiroshima was home to an imperial Japanese naval port in 1945. We should not forget the sacrifice of 100,000 innocent civilians burned to ash by nuclear bomb. If a naval base is built in Gangjeong, Jungmun, and Seogwipo could become another Hiroshima as early as 2025, when China could surpass the U.S for Northeast Asia hegemonic control. Nuclear weapons are 5,000 times more powerful today than they were in 1945. The destruction would be unfathomable.

I served in the military at the DMZ on the North-South border in the early 80s. We were instructed to regard those young North Koreans as nonhumans. So, I spent my youth trying to de-humanize and cold-heartedly pointing guns at their chests. Is that not enough? Must we now prepare to fight against our neighbors China and Japan? Is that the only option we can think of? Why not try to resolve our issues first through political or diplomatic dialogue? The logic of the blue-water Navy, one of the purposes of the construction of the Jeju Naval Base, stems from a petty imperialism spurred on by Korea's economic development. We must abandon our egotistic drive to control the wider ocean with military violence and find a more modest and practical path of international cooperation to jointly ensure ocean security. Let's not forget that it was this same expansionist arrogance and entitlement by the ROK Navy towards North Korea that led to the sinking of the Cheonan warship and the bombing of Yeonpyeong Island.

Third, the naval base construction is destroying the surrounding nature and the environment, darkening the future of Jeju Island. Jeju's natural resources and environment are its greatest asset and its most fruitful industry. Without them, no one would visit. It makes no sense to build a military base on top of an Absolute Preservation Area like Gangjeong village, just ignoring all the unique and beautiful geological features of the land. Beom Island, officially designated a natural monument, lies just 2.5 km off the coast of Gangjeong and the sea around it is a UNESCO-designated Biosphere Reserve Core Area.[1] This means that Korea has made a promise to the international community to protect and preserve this natural heritage.

---

1 UNESCO(United Nations Educational, Scientific and Cultural Organization)-designated biosphere reserves(bioregional management) refer to terrestrial, marine, and coastal ecosystem areas internationally recognized to promote conservation of biodiversity combined with sustainable use. Their main functions include conservation of biodiversity and cultural diversity and development that is socio-culturally and environmentally friendly. When Jeju Island was designated as a Biosphere Reserve by UNESCO in 2002, the Korean Government and Jeju Island promised the international community that they would preserve Jeju's natural environment.

The Ministry of Oceans and Fisheries has also designated the area a protected marine ecosystem conservation area.

Isn't it common sense not to dredge and develop military facilities in such an area inhabited by beautiful and rare creatures? I believe that keeping and protecting natural ecosystems is a shared human obligation which God has entrusted to all of humanity. Especially in this case, the site of the naval base construction is a wetland which is the habitat of the Class-2 endangered species, the red-foot crab and the boreal digging frog. The fact that official Environmental Impact Assessment did not even find or mention this, suggests just how hastily and roughshod this project has progressed. The navy now claims they will forcibly relocate endangered creatures to the nearby Yakcheonsa Temple, yet there is no one responsible for monitoring the results of the migration and the Youngsan River Basin Environmental Management Office, which has a lot of experience with such work, has stated that this manner of migration has few success cases.

Under the pretense of following regulations, the Navy is simply getting rid of the animals and plants that are obstructing their base project plan, and no one is being legally held responsible for this. The naval base construction project is a site of massacre in which humans, just one species among many in our ecosystem, arrogantly slaughter the countless other creatures that form our shared ecological fabric for its own environmental needs. Anyone who has any awareness of their own natural ecological value should oppose the tyranny of one species and the slaughter of other species in our shared ecosystem. As one of my fellow anti-naval base activists has said, "Real peace is in the place where we respect and cherish our smallest creatures." This is a sentiment we should keep in our minds.

Fourth, the Jeju Naval Base Construction Project is causing division and conflict in Gangjeong village.[2] The navy is now doing everything in their power to enforce the construction, even if it comes at the sacrifice of the entire village community. More than 50 innocent farmers, who have lived honest lives, working hard on the land, have now become criminals. They have little legal knowledge and yet have now paid over 50 million KRW in fines.[3] I, too, for the first time in my life, have been locked up behind bars. During the brutal military dictatorships of the 70s and 80s, I was a cowardly young man living in fear of the law. To atone for this, I've since worked in war zones and disaster areas around the world in places like Aceh and Haiti. Now, in the light of faith, conscience and conviction, and for the sake of justice in Korea, peace in Northeast Asia,

---

[2] Effects of the conflict on Gangjeong village from the construction of a naval base are serious. 110 Gangjeong residents participated in a mental health survey conducted by Seogwipo Shinmun newspaper. 82.6% of the surveyed reported having been involved in the campaign for or against the naval base. Of the total, 75.5% of the respondents were found to have mental health abnormalities in at least one category, with the highest reported category being hostility at 57% of respondents. Additional categories include depression (53.1%), anxiety (51%), obsessive compulsion (50%), interpersonal sensitivity (44.9%), somatization (38.8%), and paranoia (37.8%). Notably, 43.9% of respondents reported suicidal ideation in the previous week. Considering the fact that the average rate of suicidal ideation among all Jeju residents is just 8.1%, these numbers are evidences of a very serious situation. According to Dr. Lee Beom Ryong, director of Bright Neuropsychiatry, "Acknowledging the fact that we could project the maximum percentage of the general population suffering from depression to be about 20%, the present results we see in Gangjeong are severe. We cannot rule out a probability where anger may eventually be directed towards a specific object or worse, towards a specific person."

[3] As of September 2012, more than 400 people had been prosecuted, incurring fines of more than 200 million KRW.

and the protection of our ecosystem and natural environment, I will work to stop this evil, dangerous, and absurd naval base construction project.

Your Honor, a majority of Korean citizens, including residents of Jeju, and even many of those in favor of the Jeju Naval Base Construction Project, are calling for a provisional suspension of the construction to resolve ongoing conflicts among the residents first. The navy's attempt to push ahead with the construction in defiance of this public demand is based on the greed of our pro-military regime, and a general distrust of the people of this nation. If a policy initiated by the government is detrimentally affecting the lives of its citizens, then it is definitely a matter that needs reconsideration and review. The construction of the Jeju Naval Base will affect our future for generations. Is it really necessary for national security or is it foolish, dangerous, and unfounded, eventually increasing the risks to our national security? In order to end this five-year conflict, Gangjeong villagers, Jeju islanders, and people from the Korean mainland must come together and suspend this naval base construction. Before any further construction work can recommence, a thorough investigation by the Korean National Assembly must be carried out and the government must also lead conflict resolution efforts for and in the village of Gangjeong.

Lastly, I'd like to appeal to the judge for leniency, that I might undergo interrogation and investigation without physical imprisonment. I miss my loved ones and want to once again see the beautiful open sea of Gangjeong, and the green forests of Mt. Halla. I will fully participate in my investigation and trial but would like to request these be carried out without detention. I will respect the judge's recommendations and the outcome of the trial.

--Handwritten statement to appeal the suitability of arrest warrant.

July 17, 2011.

Song's appeal against his arrest was rejected. From his detention cell, He sent letters to the residents of Gangjeong village and the employees from the ROK Navy, Samsung C&T, and Daelim Construction.

Dear Residents of Gangjeong,

A cold wind blew across Gureombi when I came to Gangjeong in January. I spent the week in lonely Joongdeoksa Temple thinking of what I could do here. During my stay there, Kim Jong Hwan and Koh Jong In would visit in the evenings to lament the loss of struggle momentum in the village over a bottle of rice wine. Even when I was away, brother Jong Hwan's voice of regret lingered in my heart and ears. I thought this sorrowful voice was the voice of God. I didn't know what I had to do or could do in Gangjeong. In the face of a violent and illegal suppression of justice, it seemed that all of you were keeping silent. This silence was surely not in agreeance or compliance with the government. It seemed you had been forced to kneel and keep silent before the threat of overwhelming power. It became my job to pray for God to establish justice and make peace in Gangjeong.

I came to Gangjeong village to pray for your courage to fight for justice and hope for peace. At dawn I would go to a deserted part of the Joongdeok coast and cry out to God that the villagers would rise in strength again. I also pleaded with many pastors and priests to gather for a weekly peace prayer meeting on Gureombi. I did this because I believe everything starts from prayer. Fortunately, these things which I prayed for have now come true. You are now fighting so well. Especially I am excited by the fight of the older women of the village. You are such wonderful peace warriors. And the pastors and priests are holding regular prayer meetings and mass on Gureombi just as I first dreamed. Additionally, some members of Gangjeong Church are meeting to pray every Sunday at 5 p.m. I thank God that my prayers have been answered in abundance. However, Yang Yoon Mo and Choi Sung Hee were arrested, and now Koh Kwon Il, Chairman of the Villagers' Committee to Stop the Naval Base, and myself have been arrested. If I were afraid of being arrested, I wouldn't have started praying at the Joongdeok coast. I feel calm because I am prepared not only for justice and peace, but also for death. I will gladly accept any hardship because I am committed to you, the people of Gangjeong, and your long struggle for justice and peace, to protect our country from the devastation of war.

I respect and am proud of the residents of Gangjeong village. If we can block the construction of the naval base with the power of the people, we can save our country from future wars and prevent further atrocities from the brutal militarism that tramples our generation. You give hope not only to your fellow Koreans, but to others across the world suffering from military facilities and the threat of war. Stopping military bases through the power of the people is a rare thing in this world and the effort itself is a victory. The world's leading newspapers and broadcasts will announce the victory of Gangjeong to the world. Gangjeong is the hope of the world. We must do it. The struggle of Gangjeong village will become a message of peace that people can prevent the construction of military bases and future wars. Even if we fail, history will remember our prophetic voice of peace, and this fight for peace we've fought will surely be passed on to and praised by our descendants. I will continue to pray here in prison. I will meet you in prayer, dreaming of that day, when the naval base construction has been erased, and we all gather together to celebrate on Gureombi, holding hands, singing songs of victory.

May God aid and protect you.

Song Kang Ho
In Detention at Jeju Dongbu Police Station
July 17, 2011

To Those Involved in the Construction from the Navy, Samsung, and Daelim,

I first began to meet you in early March, as spring was just beginning. It's already been five months. I feel sorry for the troubles I have caused you. If we'd met elsewhere, not like this at the construction site, we might have become good friends. You seem like nice people. Although some of you have sworn at me and even physically restrained me, I don't hold it against you. Anyway, we didn't have a great relationship, so now as you've wished, I've been imprisoned. But I don't blame you for this. I think the misguided polices of the Korean government and the Ministry of National Defense are mainly at fault in this. On Korean Constitution Day, I was imprisoned for "Obstruction of Business" of a naval base construction project that is being enforced in disregard of the very democratic principles of our country's constitution. I was imprisoned for fighting to safeguard our democracy, to save our country from the devastation of war, and to protect our beautiful natural habitats. I care about you and even have respect for you. Maybe it's the strong respect I have for callous-handed laborers. It's also true that while I oppose war and hate militarism, when I see soldiers in formation, I often still feel a sense of human warmth and respect for their confident and dignified appearance.

I have a favor to ask you. Please don't make any more criminals. More than 50 villagers have been subjected to punishment and dozens more have been prosecuted. Please think about what these villagers are going through, and the pain and hardship that your presence has brought to a once peaceful village of fishers and farmers. Why do you have to work this way? Don't you realize that if you continue to carry out this construction by force, a greater national resistance will arise, and a larger conflict will be inevitable? I believe this lunatic construction will one day cease, but the sacrifices, pain, loss, and damage that you cause the residents to suffer will have irreversible consequences. Don't forget that some villagers may even lose their lives. Please, I am begging you. Please suspend this construction and resolve your conflict with the residents before anything else. Even the residents who are in favor of the naval construction support this demand. There is no reason for a military that despises its own people to exist. Please show them the respect they deserve as residents of the village and listen to their demands and perspectives. Stop your war on the villagers and try to persuade them with reason instead. Don't you have alternative plans and compensation proposals? Why don't you try to convince the residents instead? The residents of Gangjeong love their country and do their military service just like any other place in Korea. Appeal to their patriotism, remind them of that spirit. Please just do your best to engage in conversation with these residents.

However, one thing is clear. If you cannot convince the villagers, you must give up your plan to construct this naval base. You cannot enforce this construction through violence. To do so is to destroy the democratic identity of Korea. I am earnestly appealing to you. Please announce a suspension of construction and attempt an open dialogue with the residents. This is the only way to resolve all the conflict caused by the naval base construction and stop turning good citizens into criminals. Coercing the completion of this construction is like pushing a car with a wheel that won't turn. Eventually that car will break down. Just as a stuck wheel cannot overcome asphalt, neither will the Navy nor Samsung be able to defeat the people. Before you suffer more losses and shame, and before the villagers experience more suffering and sacrifices, I appeal to you, listen to the voices of the people.

Song Kang Ho
In Detention at Jeju Dongbu Police Station
July 17, 2011

Song Kang Ho did not halt his struggle even after being released on probation on July 28, 2011. Instead, he stood even stronger. In April of 2012, at the Gureombi demolition site, Song was arrested again after breaking through the barbwire fence around the area. During his arrest, he was ruthlessly assaulted by the police. Fr. Kim Seong Hwan witnessed the arrest and corroborated Song's own account of the violence, saying that the police treated Song "like an object," and also punched him multiple times with closed fists as they forced him into the police vehicle. However, the police officers involved in the incident, from the 7th mobile unit of the Gyeonggi Provincial Police Agency and the 32nd mobile unit of the Seoul Metropolitan Police Agency deny the accusations.[4] On April 2nd, 2012, Song filed a complaint with the National Human Rights Commission against the police involved in his arrest.

Around 2 p.m. on April 1st, during a protest against the movement of heavy construction machinery for the destruction of Gureombi rock, I

---

4 For footage related to the scene see: http://goo.gl/KON1e

was outside the barbed wire fence to the west of Gureombi shouting, "Don't destroy Gureombi! Stop the construction, stop!" I was not alone, but joined there in protest by Fr. Moon Jeong Hyeon, Fr. Kim Seong Hwan, and former Assemblywoman Hyun Ae Ja. Despite the protests of ourselves and others, construction workers continued to use two enormous excavators to split and break rocks and load them into dump trucks, about ten meters inside the barbed wire fence. Exasperated by the workers refusal to listen no matter how much we tried, I suddenly found myself pulling down the barbed wire, jumping over it, and running to the excavators to confront them. To my front, about 30 riot police with shields were blocking access to the excavators, their commanding officer grinning derisively. As soon as I crossed the barbed-wire I was isolated and surrounded by the riot police, hitting and kicking me as I tried to escape. One of the officers twisted my left hand behind my back, another violently stabbed my ear with his finger. I felt some sharp splinters of the broken rock pierce my foot. As they roughly carried me away, my head hit the rocky ground two or three times. It was around 2:30 p.m. when they threw me into a military jeep and drove me around to the main construction site entrance where a police vehicle was waiting for me.

Around a hundred villagers and peace activists tried to intervene, but the police held them back with a human wall of shields, to secure a passageway through which I was carried and violently thrown into the awaiting police vehicle. I tried to resist this unjust arrest as much as I could, but they grabbed and pulled my legs with greater and greater force. As I tried to shake them off, they dropped my upper torso and I partially fell, with my head getting wedged between the bottom of the police vehicle and the asphalt. I screamed in pain, but the police continued to pull me harder and harder. My neck and chin were caught on some metal structure on the underside of the vehicle, while my legs were being pulled forcefully by several people, and I screamed urgently. But they continued to pull harder, and I began to feel parts of my teeth grind to sand inside my mouth. I heard a loud crack sound from neck. I felt like my head was going to be ripped off my torso. Not only did they continue to pull me non-stop, but someone grabbed my genitals several times. I heard laughter from the police. I heard Fr. Kim Seong Hwan protesting their behavior.

Using adrenaline from fear and pain, I finally managed to get my jaw unstuck from beneath the vehicle. Exhausted, the police easily dragged me out and threw me in the vehicle. The police complained that I was making a mess as I spit out my bits of chipped teeth. Suddenly a police officer named "Goh" who was sitting behind me, punched me hard in the left side of my abdomen. When we got to the Seogwipo Police Station, I told them I had pain in my jaw, right shoulder, and back and asked them to call for an ambulance. As I was lying down, they mocked me saying I just looked sleepy so I should go to sleep. I pleaded with them to call the 119 emergency services, but they waited more than 30 minutes to call.

I file this complaint to the National Human Rights Commission against the police officers who arrested me. To ensure that the police will never again trample on citizens' human rights, nor threaten their lives, nor disrespect their bodies, I hereby call for a thorough investigation and disciplinary action against the police brutality I experienced.

-*Handwritten Statement by Song Kang Ho*

April 2, 2012

Song often said he had come to Gangjeong to pray. He prayed aloud every morning on Gureombi. Even after the path to Gureombi was blocked by fence and barbed wire, he would go from the sea by kayak. When kayak was not possible, he would swim. Above all else, 'warrior' Song Kang Ho was a person of prayer. He left behind his morning prayers in his room.

Our Father in Heaven,

I pray for the Gangjeong villagers who are struggling in pain and grief. God, the navy has entered this village with an evil spirit of division, and they drove these people into terrible conflict. Parents and their children, brothers and sisters, friends and relatives are fighting against each other like enemies. Father God, please have mercy on Gangjeong so that the villagers who threaten and antagonize each other can forgive one another. Guide us to walk the path of reconciliation and mutually beneficial peace. Cut off the evil schemes of the enemy that seeks to constantly divide and alienate, and let the villagers be able to meet together dozens, hundreds, countless times, without external pressure or agitation, so that they themselves might decide their own fate.

God, this naval base construction project is a criminal act against humanity, done from the very start through lies, fraud, bribery, and manipulation. That's why the majority of the villagers have opposed it from the beginning. The government and navy have not persuaded the residents, nor have they tried. They continue to push this reckless construction through coercive force, ignoring the legitimate demands and opposition of the villagers. They imprison and punish good, innocent people. Lord, please put an end to this illegal and unjust construction immediately. Replace their injustice with your justice. Please pity these innocent people, oppressed by police coercion and branded and punished as criminals by regime-corrupted judges. Judge the arrogance of those in power who spread propaganda that these exhausted villagers, silenced and groaning in frustration from their long struggle, support the base plan. Give strength to the exhausted and despairing people of Gangjeong and fill them with a just anger. Help them to never give up this righteous struggle.

God, who dares to fight against the President, Ministry of National Defense, or mega corporations like Samsung and Daelim? How can the residents of tiny Gangjeong village fight against the strong and giant government and conglomerates? But we believe and pray that you are a God who lifts up the weak to shame the strong and the ignorant to shame the wise. Jehovah God, fight against these wicked and unjust forces in place of us for we are week.

God, protect Gureombi against destruction. Rebuke the lunatics who want to blow up the natural park that is Gureombi and cover it with cement. Protect this living rock, that it might be a place of spirituality, meditation, and prayer.

God, the Joongdeok sea, where dolphins dance in front of Gureombi, is a beautiful sea inhabited by many species. Rare marine life such as Triton's trumpet sea snail, and soft coral, like the orange cup coral, live here too. Now all these creatures face annihilation by this naval base construction. God, with what authority do we, humans, massacre and expel these creatures who have lived on this land and in this sea for long before we even existed? Lord, I believe to cherish and love the lives of these tiny creatures on the brink of obliteration is defending your peace. Lord, preserve the living Gureombi ecosystem and all the living creatures off the coast of Gangjeong.

God, lead the churches of Korea to reject selfish nationalism and patriotism and worship only you, Yahweh God. Give us the faith and courage to live in a world without war and military training and "beat our swords into ploughshares and spears into pruning hooks," as the prophets dreamed. Lead us to be Christians who firmly believe Jesus Christ, the Christ who said those that live by the sword will die by the sword. Let us be Christians who prove with our bodies that Jesus Christ, who is peace himself, is also the way to peace. Christ, just as you broke your body to break down dividing walls and make peace, so let us sacrifice ourselves to break down the walls of conflict and discord and create a path for reconciliation.

God, let Jeju Island become a demilitarized peace island. Do not allow any soldiers or bases, weapon or ammunition depots, or any military facilities to set foot on Jeju Island. Do not allow any warships or weapon carrying ships to enter the coast of Jeju. Preserve the blue, clean waters of the Jeju sea.

God, inform not just the citizens of this country, but people across the world, about Jeju Island and its position at the geopolitical center of Northeast Asia. If any country militarizes or fortifies Jeju, it will inevitably intensify tensions in the region which can only lead to a dark fate for Korea. Therefore, expel all military facilities from Jeju, and let Jeju become a place of conflict meditation, dialogue, and negotiations for world peace and the co-existence of mankind. To this end, attract UN-affiliated groups like the United Nations Regional Center for Peace and Disarmament, University of Peace, and UN Security Council, and encourage diplomatic efforts for multi-party talks like the Beijing six-party talks. Bring international peace organizations to Jeju to establish headquarters and branches, one by one. May peace conferences be held which contribute greatly to peace in not just Northeast Asia, but around the world.

God, remember the innocent victims of unjust state power, mass murdered during Jeju's dark traumatic history following the 4.3 Uprising. Let the memories of this painful wound bring an awareness of history to the people of Jeju Island, to foster a desire for peace. Let peace education be taught in schools at all levels for the peace of future generations. May young people in Jeju be given a choice of not just mandatory military service, but to serve for peace in conflict areas in Korea and around the world.

God, let the people of Korea know that the nature and peace of Jeju are its most precious commodities to protect. Keep the beautiful nature of Jeju from being demolished and destroyed by military bases and polluting industries, and help Jeju to develop in balance and restraint, based on peace. Help the people of Jeju to not become slaves to materialistic greed but to seek lives of community and co-existence. Let the Jeju Sammu(three absences) tradition of a life without beggars, thieves, or gates be upheld in the midst of this capitalist society. Allow everyone to be fairly compensated for their sweat and labor, in a land without rich or poor, where all can live well.

God, help our country to follow the teachings of Kim Koo, that Korea will be strong not through military power, but through a robust and rich culture. Let us follow the dream of Ham Seok Heon to be a small but strong and peaceful, neutral country. Let us remember Reverend Moon Ik Hwan who struggled for peaceful reunification with his entire being, and Kwon Jeong Saeng who chose voluntary poverty as he desperately longed for North and South to live together. Let us follow these precious national signposts on the path to peaceful reunification.

God, may the movement for peaceful reunification spread like a flame from Mt. Halla to Mt. Baekdu and let the Jeju islanders, Koreans who yearn for justice and peace, and the citizens of the world who are in solidarity with us, unite in cooperation to bring the downfall of this unjust, wicked, naval base construction project which blocks the path to peace. Let people of peace ride peace buses, planes, boats, and bicycles, join peace marathons, cross the mountains and the seas, to gather in Gangjeong, hold hands, and stop this unrighteous naval base.

God, let the Republic of Korea be a site of freedom in this world, and country of justice and peace. Towards that end, may Jeju become a demilitarized island of peace. May the sky, land, and sea, and world, and all living things in this world, come together to block the construction of this naval base that seeks to drag our nation into the abyss of war. In the name of Jesus Christ our Lord, who was crucified and died for justice, peace, and joy, and will rise again to be with us until the end, Amen.

Song was so convinced of his innocence, that he refused bail and decided to remain in custody, pending trial. He faced his trial with resolve.

I am detained and on trial charged with violating the Punishment of Minor Offenses Act by committing "Obstruction of Maritime Construction," "Property Damage," and "Obstruction of Business." I was previously sentenced to eight months in prison and two years of probation on November 15 of last year. Although the court calls me an offender, when I came to Gangjeong, I was an ordinary citizen and had never faced any sort of legal prosecution until March of last year. I would not be a criminal if the naval base construction process had been carried out with democratic procedures and the consent of the village residents. If that were the case, I would most likely be elsewhere now, doing the work I had previously been doing, such as helping war refugees or reuniting divided families in conflict areas like East Timor, Afghanistan or Kashmir, or perhaps assisting the victims of tsunamis or earthquakes in places like Banda Aceh and Haiti.

What I have experienced in Gangjeong village is a reality where its powerless residents, who aspire to justice, have been unjustly silenced and forced to kneel before those in power. Anyone with a conscience or faith must be willing to help those who are suffering unjustly. If I'm guilty of anything, I'm guilty of standing with and assisting the wronged residents of Gangjeong.

Mr. Prosecutor, and your honor, have you ever been to Gangjeong village? Have you ever heard the cries of desolation of the farmers whose land were taken by force? Fraud, blackmail and intimidation are now rampant in Gangjeong and those who try to stop it are arrested and imprisoned in the name of the law. The coast of Gangjeong has been a badangbat(sea field)[5] for haenyeo divers for hundreds, if not thousands of years. In 2007, when around 80 of those divers were conned into selling their sea field, nature's gift to be used by their descendants for many more generations, to the navy. But those divers are not the owners of that sea field; it was merely borrowed from their descendants. The navy tricked them into selling it, promising them 100 million KRW each. And thus, Gureombi and the Gangjeong coast, the shared lands of our children and their descendants, "became" naval property.

---

5 Since the ancient times, the people of Jeju have referred to the sea as a field (for gathering sea life for sustenance and livelihood). In Jeju Island's distinct Korean dialect, badang means "sea" (Standard Korean for "sea" is bada) and bat means "field", so badangbat could be translated as "sea field."

The navy purchased more than 65 acres of land in Gangjeong. That land belonged to more than 100 landowners, of whom more than 60 were forced to sell. They merely received notices that said, "The price for your land is in the bank. Go get it." The farmers whose land was taken by force had no choice but to collect the money for their stolen land. This is an obvious injustice. They also threated exorbitant rent charges on the newly stolen land for those farmers who refused to take down their greenhouses and structures.

The navy claims to have relocated endangered plants and animals like the red-foot crab, the boreal digging frog, and the Cladium chinense Nees. But they did so carelessly and with no regard for long-term outcomes. The navy was not interested in the survival of these species from the start. Pretending to follow regulations, the navy has quickly disposed of these obstacles to their plan.

Your honor, do you know how the naval base construction in Gangjeong village came to fruition? The navy's most criminal act was when they hastily consorted with the former Gangjeong mayor resulting in the illegal village meeting on April 26, 2007, that "voted" to invite the construction of the base. In order to hurriedly manipulate public opinion, they mobilized the previously bribed female divers and a few other residents who had been bribed to favor the naval base for the meeting. This irregular village meeting was essentially navy controlled by proxy, and no adequate notice was given to the rest of the village residents. Those in attendance were blocked from expressing any objections, and the mayor conducted the vote via applause. How can such a critical decision be made so connivingly? How can such a meeting without a public hearing, free discussion, or any debate on pros vs. cons, be considered the meeting that decided the will of the residents? Such an underhanded process led to the impeachment of the village mayor and a great conflict between the villagers. The navy is building this base at the expense of our nation's constitution. Those who endanger this country are not the defendants here, but the navy who is disturbing our constitutional order.

Even more, they seek to destroy Gureombi rock, designated as Natural Monument No. 442, and part of the Absolute Conservation Area. It is being blasted mercilessly with dynamite. Is it a crime to help the residents of Gangjeong village defend their hometown, preserve the constitution of Korea, and protect our natural heritage? More than 600 innocent people have been arrested and more than 300 have been prosecuted in this small village of only 1,900 residents. Does this make any sense at all? Mr. Prosecutor, how long will you support the navy, using the innocent Gangjeong villagers and citizens who long for peace as sacrificial lambs? If the Korean court is truly just and fair, it is not we who should be on trial. It should be the navy disturbing our constitutional order, the tycoons for tax-wasting development, the police for aiding them, the governor of Jeju for abandoning his duties, and the judges of the Jeju courts for being their handmaidens.

If there exists a law without logic, then it should no longer be considered law. The Jeju courts have repeatedly made decisions on cases related to the naval base construction without any apparent logical rationale. On December 15, 2010, during the first trial regarding the "Suspension and Invalidation for the Absolute Preservation Area Change Disposition" it was ruled that the preservation of Gureombi had no direct, individual, or specific impact on the residents of Gangjeong and therefore those residents did not qualify as plaintiffs in the case. An enormous natural monument in the middle of the village, a place which all residents have cherished for generations, is blocked off by barbed wire and destroyed and this has no detrimental impact on the villagers? By this logic, no one on Jeju could stop even Mt. Halla from being destroyed.

On May 18, 2011, in yet another trial against the naval base construction, regarding the damages to the groundwater, ecosystem and natural environment of Gangjeong, the court again dismissed the villagers' claims, with the bizarre reasoning that it was the environment that was damaged not the residents themselves. By this absurd logic, the red-foot crabs or the freshwater spring or the boreal digging frog themselves are required to be the plaintiffs and sue for damages on their own? Why are these judges, some of the most intelligent individuals in Korea, making such senseless rulings? The reason is simple. Because the judges tiptoe around those with power. For the same reason, these very smart prosecutors do not want to release me on the grounds that somehow I'm a risk for both flight and recidivism simultaneously. A person who runs away is not able to repeat a crime, and the person who repeats a crime cannot also be running away. Either these prosecutors are so incompetent that they cannot understand basic logical contradictions, or they too have become servants of the powerful.

Although the Seogwipo Police are quick to arrest and prosecute Gangjeong residents, they neglect or even collude with the illegal operations of the Samsung C&T barges which have twice dropped caisson pier foundation retaining structures in Gangjeong's waters without the proper inspection certification. Every attempt by Gangjeong residents to monitor these illegal activities has been aggressively blocked by the police and coast guard. Eventually the barge captain was charged but despite his proven record of recidivism, he was not detained in anyway. Worse, the coast guard intelligence chief covered for the barge captain, lying to the Gangjeong residents that the unauthorized barge was legally operating under a temporary permit.

On the 10th of last month, the Jeju court rejected the application filed by the Gangjeong Village Association to lift the ban on outdoor demonstrations in Gangjeong. Once again, we see the Jeju court gagging the residents of Gangjeong in the name of the law. How can citizens express their concerns when they are forced to be silent when the courts prohibit freedom of assembly and expression, which are stipulated in our constitution and also the foundation of our laws? In his book, Against Democracy, Ha Seung Woo wrote, "To a tell a person who has no voice under the law, to follow the law, is violence." This point accurately reflects the reality of Gangjeong.

I got my doctorate degree in theology from Heidelberg University in Germany. I've been a theologian, a university lecturer, and an assistant pastor. For the past ten years, I have worked to aid refugees in war and disaster areas around the world. I never had a criminal record until I came up against this wicked naval base construction project in Gangjeong. Here in Gangjeong I have fought to protect democracy, which is the foundation of the constitution of the Republic of Korea, to preserve the beautiful and holy natural heritage of Gureombi, and to defend this small village community undergoing destruction. I have never assaulted nor even sworn at anyone during my protests, even when filled with anger. I keep these words of Gandhi in my heart, "You cannot win unless you treat your enemy as your family."

I believe that I am innocent. Nevertheless, taking the current political situation into consideration, the possibility of the judge condemning the navy's illegal construction project while acquitting me seems about as unlikely as a judge during the Park Chung Hee regime acquitting those who fought against the dictatorship and struggled for democracy. But I believe that one day, justice will overcome injustice and peace will overcome violence. I would also like to believe that there is someone in this court who is brave enough to deliver a fair and just verdict so that we can put an end to these witch hunts that turn innocent Gangjeong residents and peace activists into victims of the law. The navy's attempt to achieve national security at the expense of the people, is reminiscent of Hitlers' Nazism which burned his own country to ashes. The country we seek is one where people live in peace and where the justice for the powerless are upheld.

My father is 90 years-old and he often tells me that opposing the naval base construction is impossible, like hitting a boulder with an egg. He begs me to stop saying that it is a meaningless sacrifice. He may be right, but I cannot stop this seemingly impossible, reckless fight. Because as a human being, as a Korean citizen, and as a Christian, it is a just fight to protect the peaceful Gangjeong community, the sacred rock Gureombi, and the beautiful Gangjeong sea. I believe that God has allowed me to become a victim of the fight for justice rather than kneeling cowardly before an unjust strongman.

In the written indictment, the prosecutor has furiously accused me of ridiculing judicial authority under the guise of justice and peace. But the judiciary should be ashamed when it sees itself groveling before those in power, rather than having the courage to defend justice.

Your honor, I'm pleading with you to put a stop to the construction of this naval base that is turning good and innocent citizens into criminals. How many more criminals will you create? For what does the law exist? Is it to turn people into criminals or to protect them? A just judgement ends conflict and strife. Thus far, the Jeju court has not been able to deliver a fair verdict that would resolve the conflict and discord in Gangjeong village. Instead, it has caused continual frustration and disappointment to the villagers. Nonetheless, I will not give up my conviction that God's hope begins where human beings despair. I firmly believe that the future belongs to God and that God will bring about justice and peace.

Your honor, I am not asking for your mercy. I merely ask you to uphold the constitution of the Republic of Korea and deliver a just judgement.

-*Trial Statement by Song Kang Ho, May 17*

In the hot summer of 2012, on the 100th day of his detention, protests in Gangjeong and across the country called for Song's release. An art exhibition entitled, "People I Miss" was held in the Gangjeong harbor, displaying the works of Emily, a Taiwanese activist and a fellow member of both Save Our Seas maritime action team and The Frontiers alongside Song. Around that time, the Gangjeong Grand March for Peace and Life was held with around 7,000 participants from all over the country and the world. But Song was still imprisoned at the foot of Mt. Halla. Perhaps Jesus was there in the cell with him. Just like the world could not handle Jesus, neither can any prison restrain Song Kang Ho. Hope cannot be frustrated by despair.

Chapter 12

Letters and Journals from Prison

Though injustice kept his body in prison, his soul remains as free as ever. The tired body moans and the lonely heart may cry in solitude, but his unwavering hope glides him like the sea breeze in search of justice. He has always been a sailor.

April 12, 2012: "Let Us Be Comrades for Life"

Dear SOS[6] Members with whom I'm Incredibly Proud of,

I wonder what kind of change, political reform, and restructuring will come to Gangjeong following the long-awaited April 11th general elections. In prison, there's no news regarding the elections on the television, just outdated re-runs and soap operas. My unexpected imprisonment means that I was unable to vote, or even apply for an

---

6 SOS(Save Our Seas) is a group formed by activists in Gangjeong to monitor, protest, and take direct action against the navy's unlawful maritime construction.

absentee ballot. Seeing the results of the election, I lamented that politicians can rarely be trusted and I felt a sense of loneliness that no one will protect Gangjeong, unless we protect it ourselves. I have a deep distrust of politicians because for them even justice and peace can just be tools to gain power.

I hope that our SOS resistance movement at sea will gain a broader public appeal. I think it's necessary to continue our actions in a consistent manner. Once a week, it will be good to take all our boats and kayaks to the sea in a larger demonstration of our opposition, and then daily, take two or three kayaks out in protest. Just as continuous one-person protests happen at the main gate to the construction site, I think it is our responsibility to express constant opposition by the sea. If you continue to resist ceaselessly, some valuable opportunities will surely arise. This is the wisdom that history has taught us.

Of course, our Gangjeong struggle is important to us, but don't just concern yourselves with Gangjeong. We must remember that our fight is not just against the Jeju Naval Base Construction Project but against the entire military-industrial complex that creates war and conflict for profit and power. This is an enormous struggle fought by countless comrades across this country and around the world. Thus, our fight in Gangjeong is inextricably linked to the struggles against military facilities in places like Pyeongtaek, Okinawa, Diego Garcia[7], and the Spratly Islands.[8]

It is my hope that SOS can be warriors in the global anti-war peace movement against the specter-of-violence-possessed murderers of this world. I want to share my hope and vision with you, but please don't misunderstand, I do not have political ambitions. That's why I can be brave enough to make these crazy suggestions to you. We have to believe that a small minority can change the world, and that we can be that minority. The disciples who followed Jesus were only a small group of twelve, but they were really the Kingdom transition team. At first, they confused the Kingdom of Jesus with

---

7 Diego Garcia is a British-controlled island leased to the U.S. for use as a military base. Because of its strategically valuable location in the middle of the Indian Ocean, it has played a major role in U.S. Military expansion into Africa, Middle East, and South Asia, especially during the Gulf War and the Iraq War. The base and its history were not widely known before the 1990s, when a number of shocking revelations have come to light about the mistreatment of the island's original Chagossian inhabitants by the U.K. and the U.S. From 1968-73, the Chagossians were forcibly expelled from the island. Initial deportation strategies applied increasing pressure on the residents in order for them to leave "willingly." Such tactics included a ruling that anyone who left the island for any reason would not be permitted to return. Another tactic included the mass slaughter of more than 1000 islander pet dogs in 1971. Between 1971-73, the remaining islanders were forcibly removed, often packed onto over-capacity cargo ships and dumped on other foreign islands like Mauritius and Seychelles. Although eventually some residents received compensation totaling around 6,000 USD per person, they have never been allowed to return to their homes and many live in poverty on the margins of the societies they were forced to immigrate to. Various rulings, including by the International Court of Justice in The Hague have favored the Chagossians, but the U.K. and U.S. governments continue to block the return of the Chagossians to their homeland.

8 Spratly Islands are an archipelago situated at the southern tip of the South China Sea. It is a group of islands consisting of 18 main small islands and more than 100 reefs. It is one of the main territorial disputes in East Asia. The islands are rich in oil and natural gas, and they are a key location for maritime traffic and commercial fishing. The surrounding countries, the Philippines, Malaysia, Brunei, Vietnam, China, and Taiwan, all hold competing claims to sovereignty in the area and over the area's resources. As the various claimants also deploy military forces to the islands to keep them under control, the risk of armed conflict is always present.

secular kingdoms or secular power. We are also a Kingdom transition team. This is not one of secular power, but a kingdom of peace, justice and joy. Friends, this possibility breathes inside of you. You, who I met off the coast of Gangjeong, can change the world just like those fishermen of Galilee turned the world upside down. You are more than capable. Of course, the path will be long and the struggle hard, but the fruits of our labor will be invaluable to peace in the world.

Let's go to Sulawesi together when I am released. Let's catch fish in the clear, warm sea, and talk about the beauty of life while watching the dark red sunset. Let's dream together on a pitch-black night, beneath a blanket of stars. It has been my hope for a long time to go together with you to sail on the seas of Indonesia, with the dream that our comrades and co-workers could become like the descendants of Abraham, "as numerous as the stars in the sky and countless grains of sand."

What is Gangjeong to us? It is just one of the fights we will face. Unlike our long-time warrior sister Duhee, this may be the first battle some of you, younger people, have fought. Do your best, and fight to win. But don't forget that we have many battles to fight. Let us be comrades for life. Let's be the transition team for the Kingdom of real power, where love and truth meet and justice and peace kiss. Thank you for your love and care. It won't be long until we see each other again. Let's prepare to meet each other. Justice must prevail! Persevere until the end!

From a small room at the foot of Mt. Halla

Yours truly, "Water Spirit"

April 19: Cloudy, "4.19"

I'm not sure if anyone in our generation remembers the day the foundation of our democracy was laid. The future of democracy in Korea seems as gloomy as today's weather. I've heard that many in Gangjeong village are still struggling endlessly, getting arrested and being detained, but unfortunately the national and Jeju governments continue to support the navy and its plans. This morning during visiting hours, I was visited by Fr. Moon Jeong Hyeon, Rev. Song Yeong Seop, "Silver," "Seahorse," and my wife. Fr. Moon was wearing a cast on his right arm. I greeted him with a deep bow. He has taken many perilous paths throughout his life, and I was so grateful to see him still alive. I teared up to hear that he had come directly to visit me after being discharged from Jeju National University Hospital. I hurt for this priest who had just narrowly escaped death.[9] Who cannot see the pain he has suffered and that is in his heart?

My lawyer also visited me today to suggest merging another

---

[9] Fr. Moon Jeong Hyeon is a well-known, long-time activist and priest in Korea. On April 6th, the Good Friday, Fr. Moon and others were conducting a Stations of the Cross Catholic prayer ceremony and mass around the boundaries of Gureombi and the construction site. The fourteenth and final station was on the end of the southern pier of Gangjeong Harbor. Overzealous coast guard and police began to block and interfere, and a struggle dangerously ensued atop the giant concrete breakwater tetrapods at the end of the pier. During this struggle Fr. Moon fell between a gap in the tetrapods and plunged seven meters to the concrete below, losing consciousness. Presumed near death or in critical condition, he was rushed to the hospital, where he regained consciousness but was told he might be required to stay and be treated for six months. However, a few days later, bandaged but already on the mend, he left the hospital, visited Song in prison, and headed straight back to Gangjeong village.

case with my present one and by doing so, perhaps reduce my final sentence. I said I'm not interested in long or short sentences; I want to be defended as innocent and to prove the injustice and illegality of the naval base construction project. Of course, the judge would never hand down such a verdict. My only hope is that through these court battles, the problems of the naval base and all those that profit from it will be clearly exposed. There is no reason to work to reduce my sentence or even have a trial at all, unless it has some effect on these judges and their courts, who have suppressed justice, peace, democracy and freedom in the name of the law. However, the trial will have value if MINBYUN(Lawyers for a Democratic Society) who has taken my case, is willing to fight against the naval base construction project. History will one day evaluate these corrupt and unjust judges, and just lawyers and judges can bring that day closer to us. If these lawyers are truly willing to stand in court to bring voice to these victims and save our cultural and natural heritage from destruction, then I am willing to stay in prison for 1,000 days.

May 6: "Learning Democracy in a Tiny Prison Cell"

There was a changeover in our cell, with several cellmates leaving and some new inmates taking their place. One of the new inmates, also the youngest, is affiliated with a gang. When I returned from court, the atmosphere in the cell was uncomfortable and tense. This young, new inmate had taken the best spot, next to the window, and had re-arranged the space. He had also taken down all our towels from the shared towel rack and hung up only his own. The inmate who had previously been the most powerful in the room, normally a very talkative person, sat quietly in the corner. That night when preparing for bed, the newcomer tried to order and threaten the others, again creating a tense and uncomfortable situation. He even threatened an elderly inmate for his snoring. That night a heavy silence hung over the cell, and I slept poorly. It is not easy for 6 or 7 people to have a peaceful relationship, especially in such a small space. Obviously, something needs to change in this situation.

The next day the young gang member brought up that our room was not functioning to his liking. He said that we are not following gang-approved prison traditions as we should be doing. Prisoners affiliated with gangs in prison often try to govern others through coercion and fear. They make newcomers do all the chores and threaten those who refuse. They try to create a strict hierarchical and military-like atmosphere. There is also a lot of bullying and hazing involved, such as forcing other inmates to only eat others' leftovers, or blocking them from using the toilet, and generally making things miserable. It's obviously not desirable for an already miserable prison life, and fortunately the other cellmates, veteran prisoners with lots of prison experience, strongly disagreed and asked me to reject this suggestion. Although there was some further trouble with this young cellmate, he was soon transferred to another cell.

Fortunately, the other inmates wanted to continue our small democracy experiment in our cell. It wasn't always easy to do, but we openly discussed issues during meetings together and took turns with chores. Some of the long-time inmates felt embarrassed or discomfort at our strange new style of prison life, but most of the inmates created an atmosphere of respect. Unfortunately, people are always coming and going from our cell, so we have to fight to maintain that atmosphere. Even in prison, it's possible to create and maintain a small democratic order. I'm deeply grateful to all the inmates of our cell. Especially for "senior" inmates who were willing to do burdensome chores without forcing weaker or younger inmates to do them. As well as those inmates who tolerate inmates who snore.

May 23: "Those Big Fat Churches and Their Many Members"

Dear Park Jung Kyung Soo,

Brother Kyung Soo, I am at peace here in prison. However, my heart feels heavy when I think about the challenges and hardships the Gangjeong residents experience in their daily lives as they fight against unjust powers. I feel a little guilty that I'm the only one able to enjoy a bit of selfish peace in prison. Prison life confines my life to a space the size of a matchbox, where there is no cool, fresh air or warm sunlight. Due to my daily habit of praying every morning on Gureombi, I find myself waking up very early here in prison as well. When the sun rises and casts its light through the prison bars, reminding me of the reality of my confinement, I wake up and kneel on the floor to pray. I pray for the destruction of Gureombi to cease, for peace and comfort to come to the shattered Gangjeong community, for beautiful Jeju Island to become a demilitarized island of peace, and for the peace movement to spread like flames across the nation from Mt. Halla to Mt. Baekdu.

I remember visiting you when you were in Seongdong Detention

Center a few years ago. My eyes filled with tears as we met separated by iron bars. In a system that forces the most precious years of youth to be wasted through meaningless military service, I felt as though you were locked up on behalf of all young people in Korea who want to live by their faith and conscience. I am so angry that our country is a barbaric nation that can only punish young people who choose to practice their God-given freedom of conscience.

I have a dark family past from a long time ago that my relatives want to hide. One of my distant relatives was a Jehovah's Witness. He was imprisoned, beaten, and tortured for refusing to serve in the military. Finally, he couldn't take it anymore and took revenge on the soldiers who had abused him, shooting and killing several of them. He was tried and sentenced to death. All involved in this tragedy, including those young soldiers he killed, are victims of war and the military.

It is heartbreaking to see young people trying to keep their faith and beliefs only for them to be imprisoned and suffering from state violence. It seems like just yesterday that I used to visit conscientious objectors like you. But now, the tables have turned. I remember someone once telling me that once you've sent off a few missionaries at the airport it's likely for you to become a missionary yourself sooner or later. I guess the same thing goes for visiting those in prison. If you visit enough prisoners of conscience, maybe one day they will be visiting you.

The prison yard is a place of learning. The prison's high walls are like the barriers we have in our minds. The walls around our beliefs are difficult to climb over. It's hard to break away from the conventional wisdom that a person who went to prison is a person who did something bad. Christians are no exception. But if you look back at Christian history, both Jesus and his disciples were convicts and law breakers. Christians in the early church often endured imprisonment as an inevitable hardship. Many of our countrymen will say those believers in the past were persecuted for their faith, but there is no more persecution now because we have freedom of religion in Korea. This raises the question of what faith really is. Yes, today's state no longer prohibits religious worship, prayer, bible reading, or attending church. But it's a different story when you begin to practice what you prayed for or learned at Church and from reading the Bible. The practice of faith invites us into complex social interactions that go beyond personal courtesy or service. You obviously know what I'm trying to say because you refused to serve in the military to practice the biblical teachings against killing and Jesus' words, "Love your neighbor as yourself." As a result, you were forced to spend eighteen months in prison. I hope we can talk sometime about conscientious objection again later.

If Christians fear imprisonment, they have no choice but to contain their practice of faith within the walls of the church. As a result, it seems that today's young Christians are becoming disconnected from the urgent and enormous historical task of peaceful reunification. Now our churches are bloated but these big fat churches and their many members contribute very little to the changes needed in our society. The same goes for the Buddhists. If they really practiced

Buddha's fundamental teachings which prohibit killing, they would not join the army and war would disappear. But Buddhism is similarly lethargic in the face of state power. Instead, we have Buddhist chaplains in the military, so what else can be said?

I hope that young Christians can practice their faith and conscience without fear of the law and punishment like you. Of course, it takes courage. We must ask God for courage to defeat our fears if we are to practice justice and peace against violence and wrong. And we will experience solitude through such prayers. We are preparing to take the rough and narrow path, and it will feel lonesome. Those who follow after truth and justice are inherently lonely.

When you heard that The Frontiers, who have run schools for reconciliation and peace in various conflict zones around the world, were participating in the movement against the naval base, you told me it seemed like a big change for us. In fact it is like two sides of the same coin. Here, war is approaching. Even if the work looked a little different than now, for the past decade or so, The Frontiers have focused on preventing war and making peace within those conflict zones. Before now, we worked in different countries with refugees suffering post war. In the anti-naval base movement in Gangjeong we are now working in this country to prevent war before it starts. While none of it is easy, it seems this domestic peace activity is proving a bit more difficult because we must work against our own government. When we carried out peace work in other countries, we were praised and supported in Korea. But when we do that work here, we are criticized for being anti-government.

Jesus' warning regarding specks and logs in one's eyes seems apt when talking about the state. We are easily angered by the evils of other countries like North Korea and Japan but refuse to recognize the sins of our own country. I do not believe that my country, the Republic of Korea, is more just or peaceful than other countries. The Korean government protects the interests of the powerful and rich first, and the judiciary follows suit as its loyal servant. The state's favor toward the powerful has intensified under the current regime headed by supposedly "Christian" president. In Gangjeong, more than 600 innocent residents have been arrested and more than 300 have been prosecuted, revealing the true face of this vicious Korean government behind a mask of righteousness. In such a situation, the good citizen who tries to help their suffering neighbor is considered a criminal and thrown in prison.

A peacemaker has no choice but to live a precarious life walking on top of prison walls. In 2003, I visited a peace organization in the U.S. called Christian Peacemaker Teams (CPT) which works with victims of war in places like Iraq and Colombia. One day, Gene Stoltzfus, the director at the time and someone who has since passed away, was driving me through the city. He pointed to the left side of the car and said, "All of our CPT members have lived in this house." When I looked to where he was pointing, there was an enormous, tall red brick wall I could barely see over, with another large building behind it. It was so big I couldn't see both ends at the same time. I looked questionably at the house, wondering how this small poor peace group could afford such a place to live. A moment later, our car passed the front entrance, and we both laughed together when I finally saw the large stone sign that told me we were driving by a Chicago prison.

I once gave a lecture to an IVF(Inter-Varsity Fellowship) gathering and a young man ask me the question, "Why do many young people decide to devote themselves to Christ when they are young, but gradually fade away as they get older?" I replied, "Because they lack the experience of the suffering that comes from practicing their faith." Suffering can include physical pain, material loss, and restraint of freedom. Faith that is not disciplined by meaningful hardship is easily given up or compromised in the face of threat and temptation.

There were more questions in the letter you sent me, but I'll have to answer them next time as I'm out of paper. Today my stories stayed in the prison yard. But through the bars of this prison, I can see Mt. Halla, where the greenery is getting thicker by the day. Spring is almost over; I hope you take care of your health during the change of seasons. Peace be with you.

Yours truly, Song Kang Ho from Jeju Prison

May 29: "About Jae Ho"

I just took my last hot bath for the season. Hot baths will be available again in Autumn, but I don't know if I'll still be in here then. Jae Ho (pseudonym) and I scrubbed each other's backs. Jae Ho is a young man in his twenties. He was sentenced to seven years for killing his father but is currently appealing. As I scrubbed his back, I wondered if his father used to do this when he was alive. He reminded me of my son, Han Byeol. Jae Ho, too, might have been thinking of his own father. He looked so young and naive that no one would have imagined that he had killed his own father. How could a father-son relationship end up in such a tragedy? What if it had been my own son? What if my son had a father like Jae Ho's father? I feel pity for this lonely son who killed his father and orphaned himself.

June 3: "Prison Journal, Prison History"

Yesterday morning around seven o'clock, a fight broke out between two inmates in our cell. The fight started after an older inmate complained that a younger inmate had taken his coffee mug. The upset younger inmate started yelling at other random inmates, telling them to do this or that. They began raising their voices and swearing at each other, and despite being sent to the disciplinary office, they couldn't resolve their problem. So, they were separated and transferred to different cells. The older inmate was our unofficial cell leader and when he left, he took all the snacks that he had bought with him. He even took snacks that others had bought together to share. Everyone was upset and annoyed and had nothing to eat all weekend.

A gloomy atmosphere lingered in our cell. But it instigated a conversation for nominating a new cell leader. The veteran prisoners insisted that I be the cell leader. They felt like the younger inmate who had started the fight did so because he wanted to be the cell leader and they were worried that if he became the cell leader there would be continuous trouble in our cell. Also, if there is no leader in a cell, then gang members in other cells will try to install a gang member leader, or a new prisoner with gang affiliation might come to the cell and take control.

Eventually, I decided to accept their nomination and become the cell leader. But I accepted on the condition that there would be no more hierarchy, no more privileges for seniority, and a fair distribution of washing dishes, cleaning, and chores, with no exceptions. Additionally, I said we would have a weekly meeting to handle any complaints or suggestions. I also warned them, if anyone causes a fight or breaks these rules, they will be asked to transfer cells. We even made a chore roster and attached it to the wall. Someone sarcastically commented, "Model cell," but I didn't mind. There is always a mix of mistrust and expectation when it comes to something new. The younger inmate who had caused trouble complained about his bedding once that weekend, but it didn't escalate further. That weekend, during the times when TV wasn't available, my cellmates conversed with each other a lot. They talked about prison life, military experiences, and at night, women. I sat in the corner and listened and read books, but it was too noisy and distracting to write. The last paragraph of Ha Seung Woo's book Against Democracy came to mind and I reflected upon how to practice it.

Without instruction, people tend to sit in circles to have meetings, as if by instinct. As time goes by, regulations get autonomously drawn up. The act of gathering together like this, to share ideas and create regulations, allows us to see the world a bit wider and build our strength. What we need now is to meet together sitting in a circle.

I started writing this "prison diary" yesterday. I'm going to record the stories of these people who share this tiny prison cell with me. Even in this small cell, peace is necessary, and it must be a place where people can live. I think this is a small practice of the ecumenical movement. The word "ecumenical" derives from the Hellenic Greek oikumene, and from oikumene, oikos means "home", "inhabit", or "dwell". This small cell should be a place where people can live, and human dignity is respected. I wrote the following in the introduction to my prison journal: "People in the world call prisons the bottom of society. But there are still people here. There are still histories to record."

I've been stubbornly putting off shaving my beard, but I think I might cut it after all. I feel a responsibility as the cell leader to these young inmates. I didn't really want to, but am I not a servant? A person who is made a servant by compulsion is a slave, but one who chooses to serve others is truly free. In my mid-fifties, I've become the servant of a group of low-ranking convicts in a tiny cell. I have mixed feelings about this.

June 28: "We've Lost Our Way"

A Letter to Oh Seok Jun, Editor-in-Chief of the Jeju People's Daily News.[10]

Reading the June 18th column by editor-in-chief Oh Seok Jun, for the anniversary of your publication, I was struck by the phrase, "last two years have felt like twenty years." This was heartbreaking to hear, as I

---

10 For the original letter in Korean, see: http://goo.gl/NvDUw

know these times are hard for reporters in Jeju who want to report the truth. I am currently in prison custody for my work against the naval base construction in Gangjeong village. I am a regular reader of your paper here in Jeju Prison. I subscribe to you because it is the only newspaper in the province that really reports on the sorrows of the Gangjeong residents suffering from the naval base construction. Although this is a bit late, I sincerely congratulate you on the first two years of your publication and I hope that it will remain a newspaper that will shine the light of truth on the tears and sweat of citizens suffering in darkness.

I am a "land" outsider, who came here because of my love for Jeju Island. But my naive love for Jeju was based on a lie. The lie is that Jeju is a "Special Self-Governing Province" and an "Island of Peace." In 2005, I was involved in building a house for homeless orphans and elderly people following the deadly Tsunami in Banda Aceh, Indonesia that killed more than 140,000 people. Banda Aceh had been fighting for independence since the end of World War II. The people of Aceh were exhausted from sixty years of guerrilla warfare and desperately wished for peace, and thus people were excited by the message that a peace agreement with the Indonesian government had been signed. The Guerrillas hiding in the mountains returned home, and publicly destroyed their weapons. Many of them had been away from their homes for half their lives, and now they returned on tour buses. The aspirations and hopes of the Aceh people could succinctly be condensed to a single word: "peace." People spoke warmly of the "Aceh Spring" of peace. Then at the same time came exciting news that Jeju, where 30,000 innocent citizens were once murdered by their own government, had been designated an island of peace. I decided to visit Jeju Island when I got back to Korea and soon, I became a resident of Jeju.

However, Jeju Island was not the island of peace that was promised. In particular, the land and sea of Gangjeong village had been forcibly taken from the residents to build a huge naval base with no rational reasoning behind it. The "Island of Peace" designation has been diluted to the more vague "Island of Peace and Prosperity." The scholars who once declared that the peace island should be demilitarized now argue that peace islands and military bases are compatible. Academics who do now stand for something easily jump on bandwagons, and politicians without principles or philosophy are easily swayed by those in power. Jeju Island is adrift with scholars, politicians and judges who've led us astray. But even in this grim reality, there is a glimmer of hope. On the 8th of last month, Ko Je Ryang along with Jeju National University professors, Shin Yong In, Ko Chang Hoon, and Yang Gil Hyun presented intelligent suggestions during the "What are the Alternatives to the Naval Base?" debate, arguing that "peace and nature" are the absolute values of Jeju Island.

Unfortunately, the Jeju of today, stuck in the dark quagmire of security logic, does not heed voices like these. Conscientious and honest voices like these have now become marginalized when it comes to important issues facing Jeju Island. For the past decade or so, I've been involved in the leadership of an international peace organization, and I've learned that leadership demands right judgement, a clear vision for the future, and the ability to bring harmony. In Jeju Governor Woo Guen Min, I see a total absence of leadership and a severe lack of any of these abilities. Jeju's decision to accept the naval base did not stem from right judgement. The naval base is not good for Jeju Islanders, nor is it good for national security. Governor Woo has made the wrong decision to re-subordinate the "Special Self-Governing Province" of Jeju to the Korean national government and military, turning this safe and peaceful island into a target of war, and pouring cement atop beautiful absolute preservation areas and natural monuments. As Professor Shin Yong In has pointed out, the Jeju government's short-sighted policy of chasing after anything that can make money, has no vision for the future. As the old saying goes, "A people without a vision will perish." This is the reality of Jeju Island. To win the favor of Jeju voters, Saenuri Party Rep. Park Geun Hye promised that Jeju Island would become the Hawaii of Korea, but Hawaii is not the right vision for Jeju. We have destroyed our beautiful nature and communities by following these false illusions, these mirages, sold to us by politicians. This is the same story of anxiety, pain, and anger of citizens hurt by the Four Major Rivers Project and the forced construction of nuclear power plants around Korea.

In order to find our way back and revive Jeju Island, the residents, national government, provincial government, and corporations need to meet together and start a dialogue. We must open the doors of communication again. The navy must drop its wicked patriotism-wrapped belief that a small village can be sacrificed for the sake national security. If that happens, the Gangjeong residents will have to learn to let go of their frustration and anger over what they have suffered. Samsung and Daelim must first halt their construction to participate in this conversation. They need to carefully consider how corporations might move beyond material greed and profit, to make social contributions. Provincial Governor Woo Geun Min, should not be cowardly, bending to the will of central powers. Instead, he should stand as a true representative of Jeju residents, regaining his own dignity by upholding the dignity of the residents.

In the small village of Gangjeong alone, already more than 600 citizens have been arrested, and more than 300 prosecuted. Dozens of people are still pending trials results. We must turn around, and not follow this road of incarcerating and fining innocent civilians. Let's start a new conversation to determine a better and more righteous path forward for all of us together. Let's refuse to say it's too late. If we do not turn around now, we may fall into an abyss from which we cannot return.

Sincerely,

Song Kang Ho, former director of The Frontiers, a non-profit organization

July 1: "Truth is the Strongest"

It has been three months since I was thrown into this prison. The seasonal rain front has moved north, and the hot and humid summer has come. Mt. Halla is almost always hidden by thick clouds and cannot be seen. Sometimes, I can see the foot of the mountain appearing from behind the clouds, catching a glimpse of its greenery.

I re-read Inger Aicher-Scholl's The White Rose (Die Weisse Rose).[11] It is the heartbreaking story of Munich University students who resisted the Nazi regime. Somehow, Hitler's Nazi Germany and today's Korea have a shared regression of democracy.

The book writes about some of the promises which Hitler made to the people of Germany: "He promised to work for the greatness, prosperity and welfare of the nation. He promised food and jobs, and to work hard until all could live an independent, free and happy life." But the Scholls' father taught his children about the conflict and suffering that the German people endured after the arrival of Hitler. "This is a war. It's a war between the people of the same country who have lived in peace. It is a war that takes away the happiness and freedom of each and every child who has no power to resist. It's a terrible sin." I have heard similar statements many times from Gangjeong residents. We are living the same reality which Hans Scholl spoke of, "On the surface, the house is beautiful and clean, but a scary and frightening reality is found locked in the basement of that house." This is the reality of Korea, behind the government's greenwashed mask of the Four Major Rivers Project, the Ara Canal, the Han River Renaissance, are the horrible realities of the Yongsan

---

11 The White Rose were Munich University students who fought for freedom against the Nazi regime. They were one of the first organizations to form a resistance group and systematically rebel against Nazi fascism. While most German citizens had lost the courage to resist, the students of The White Rose criticized the regime and their 'war machine' administration, printing and handing out thousands of leaflets. Among their leaders, students Christoph Probst, Hans Scholl, his sister Sophie Scholl, as well as philosophy professor Kurt Huber were executed in 1943. In Germany, their stories are used to teach young people the value of human rights and democracy.

disaster, and the workers of Hanjin Heavy Industries and Ssangyong Motors. For us, like those young people of Munich, world is often strange, lonely, and a land abandoned by God. Our experiences are alike.

The state should never be an end in itself. The existence of a state only gains its significance as a contract that exists to achieve human purposes. If its constitutional system denies the development of the spirit, it is detrimental and must be rejected." Hans Scholl's reflection is also our aspiration. "When will this country realize that the humble happiness that millions of ordinary people crave is more precious than anything else? When will this country escape the yoke of blind national ideology that tramples on ordinary, everyday life? When will we realize that living peacefully together is greater than winning on the battlefield?" All of the above are implicitly included in the first line of the White Rose's third leaflet: "The welfare of the people is the supreme law"(Salus publica suprema lex).

The records of newspapers at that time are also reminiscent of the current reality in Korea. "The newspaper… plays a role in driving people's minds into darkness. They don't report on the death sentences and the mass deaths occurring in wars. They do not see what lies behind the prisoners' pale faces. They do not hear the sound of their heartbeats, and their silent cries resounding across Germany."

Hans Scholl was also cynical towards his own Christian contemporaries. "I don't understand why pious people today fear the existence of God. This may be due to guilt at shameful acts like wielding the sword. We should be afraid of the kind of life where one is simply surviving, but not living. Because survival will disregard life."

Hans Scholl could never forget his father's wish. "Son, I want you to live your life freely and firmly, even if the road is rough." I want my children to live like this as well. Scholl was executed at the age of 24. He inscribed the following words on the prison wall: "I will live firmly against all violence." It was a phrase from Goethe that his father used often. Sophie Scholl, Hans' younger sister, was also executed, at the age of 21.

Hitler and his Nazi regime drove not only Germany, but the whole of Europe into a furnace of horror. His wretched reign caused the downfall and death of many innocent lives. However, the souls of these young people who faced tragic deaths can live on in our hearts. Truth may seem fragile, but it is the opposite. Through even a single person, truth can exert its power. But if there is no one to testify to the truth, the world remains in the dark. Each and every one of us must live as if we are the last witness to the truth. In his final statement before execution, Professor Huber concluded with the words of Philosopher Johann Gottlieb Fichte:

And you must act as though
On you and on your deeds alone
The fate of German history hung,
And the responsibility - your own.

Doesn't this echo in our ears, we, who are to light a candle of hope in an age of darkness?

July 6: Cloudy after a sunny day, "Three Gifts"

Every night I wake up to a gust of wind blowing outside. Worrying that the strong winds might blow away my laundry, I get up to check it. There are three gifts that I am grateful for here in prison. They are all things that come from outside. One is sunlight. In the early morning, the sun rising from the east shines a red beam on the south wall, and in the late afternoon, the setting sun, shines its red light from the west onto the north wall. If I sit with the sunlight on my face like a child, a sliver falls upon my face. The color is warm. The second gift is the wind. A cool breeze from Mt. Halla enters between the prison bars, swirling around the room, and slipping out towards the west corridor. I'm grateful that the fresh wind rustles our towels and dishrags hanging in our cell. The third gift is the sound of birds singing outside the window, even before dawn. The birds sing, "We are alive!" to us, to wake the dawn and let us know we've survived the night. People say the prison is full of dirty, musty air. I think this refers more to the general atmosphere of depression that permeates the cell. I suppose when you've got hundreds of inmates, convicted of countless crimes like robbery, rape, murder, fraud, drugs, and assault, and you pack them all into tiny dark cells, clean air and positive energy are not really expected to be in abundance. Nevertheless, these gifts from the outside comfort us and remind us that we're still alive.

Still, I am definitely in a better situation than my cellmates. I don't feel lonely because my wife, colleagues, and friends visit often, and I receive letters and postcards almost every day. I've learned that a ten-minute visitation can be enough to fill my heart like balloon for the rest of the day. It's still surprising to me how it will make the day pass filled with excitement, almost like a drug-induced high. The 9th will be my 100th day of imprisonment. I look at the calendar each morning and every evening I check off each day that passed. I want to be free. It is unfair that I have been unjustly deprived of my freedom. These feelings of unfairness and anger must be what makes the air in the room so stuffy. All the good things in prison come from the outside. As I sit, the hot day passes, and cool air enters through the window. Thank you.

July 8: Cloudy, "The Most Beautiful Song in the World"

The Supreme Court has once again driven Gangjeong residents to despair, rejecting the cases put forward, highlighting the injustice of the naval base construction plan. It seems like a grim sign for my trial and future. Fellow member of The Frontiers, Dong Won, will be transferred to this prison tomorrow. Although he will be closer to me, we will probably be kept separate and its unlikely for us to meet often. I detest this twisted world, where a peace-loving, good young man like Dong Won has to be confined in a dreary prison behind iron bars. In Hong Se Hwa's book The Sorrow of the Villain, there appears this heartbreaking passage:

"It was around that time that I learned about 'the most beautiful song in the world.' A French friend gave me a magazine article with picture of an elderly man with an article entitled, 'The Most Beautiful Song in the World.' In the late 1930s, Spanish leftists were driven out by Franco, forcing them to cross over the Pyrenees. Not knowing when Franco's dictatorship would end, more than 20,000 Spaniards were forced to live in exile in France. Time passed quickly…10 years, 20 years, 30 years passed. The young became old, and one by one they were buried in that other land by the hands of their comrades. And the old man with the white beard in the picture says, 'It's possible that our lives have failed, but we have sung the most beautiful song in the world. I can close my eyes in peace just with that memory.'"

Yes. It's possible that we are perhaps failing in Gangjeong. As has been the case thus far in Gangjeong, injustice may once again bring justice to its knees and violence may trample peace. However, we are now singing 'the most beautiful song in the world' in Gangjeong. We're surrounded by this beautiful music even as we're assaulted, dealt injustice, arrested, and thrown in prison. The sweet song of justice and peace surrounds us. So, let's keep failing. A failure that doesn't give up comes from a will that does not surrender or collapse. With hope and belief that justice will eventually prevail, let's rise again even if we fall seventy times seven. If we can evict the naval base from Gangjeong within two or three years, then Gangjeong will only have been able to accumulate the peace experiences of the past decade. But if the naval base is built in Gangjeong, Gangjeong could become a school that fosters peace activists for the next hundred or even thousand years. It may be painful, but perhaps that is God's path. I don't want to walk down this long road of suffering either. But what else can we do if God is the one who guides our path and steps?

I've met many Jehovah's witnesses here in prison. Most of them are conscientious objectors. They are good-natured and sincere people who volunteer for and care for other inmates. Sometimes my cellmates read their monthly magazines and brochures like "The Watchtower" and "Awake." Jehovah's witnesses seem to regard the prison as their mission field or as a faith training school. Many of the prisoners here are interested in faith and religious topics. Some of them read the bible eagerly and then argue and discuss it with each other. The questions they ask vary, but generally boil down to the essentials. "What is real Christianity?" As I was often expected to answer some of those questions, I came up with some simple responses. Real faith is, first of all, a faith that abandons greed. Greed, trying to own more even by taking from others, is never from God. Second, true faith is not arrogant. Even if you have some magical ability to cure diseases or perform miracles, if you are not humble, your arrogance will overcome your heart and lead you away from God. Third, it is a state of mind that does not seek glory or show itself off. Jesus was always wary of the dangers of showing himself and gaining popularity. It is a dangerous temptation to seek fame.

Reflecting on these responses I think most of the faiths and religions which surround us are fake, and that their faith will not save them. It is not a matter of whether one is going to heaven or not, but such faiths are separate from and have no relation with God. God does not know them.

July 26th: "Life as a Bonus"

This morning, Gangjeong elders Yoon Sang Hyo, Cho Yong Hoon, and Song Nami, came to visit me along with Kim Seong Han and Cho Je Ho. It was both heartbreaking and joyous to again meet these Gangjeong elders who are imprinted on my memory. I also felt sorry that my circumstances required these busy elders to visit this prison. Song Nami is the best friend of Gangjeong villager Jeong Young Hee. She is always cheerful and kind. She also enjoys singing and dancing. She apologized for not having visited me sooner. I was also happy to see that the villagers' faces did not look too downcast. The residents of Gangjeong deserve to be proud of their struggle of more than five years. What other village in our country has selflessly fought so hard to desperately protect the land? It's uncommon. They have continuously impressed me with their persistent and unyielding spirit, even in the face of the most adverse circumstances.

The first face I saw enter the visitation room was that of Kim Seong Han, wearing a T-shirt with my face on it. I welcomed him happily. I'm so thankful to friends who don't forget to visit me here. On his chest was an image of me taken during a protest at sea. He urged me to not reject my trial but to join it as part of the struggle. Cho Je Ho thanked me for my part in the struggle and told me I had his respect. I'm not a man worthy of such respect. I'm someone to be reproved and blamed by others.

I also received a visit from my lawyer, Kwon Young Guk. He apologized that he had tried to come sooner on several occasions but had not been able to make it till now. He was short in stature and looked like a very serious person. He began calmly sharing about his past, about covert organizing for the labor movement in the defense industry which led to an 18-month stint in prison and how even though he was often frustrated by the unfair legal system, he continues to fight using legal avenues.

> He told me that he had once refused a trial. During the Yongsan Incident, he was part of the 13-member defense team. The defense team demanded that the prosecution publicly disclose their 3,000 pages of investigation records and reports. They also argued that the trial process was biased on multiple grounds and opposed the continuation of the trial. But eventually a new defense team took the case. Lawyer Kwon felt that the judge in my case might be somewhat impartial, so I suggested that we don't reject to stand trial but to go to court and fight. I talked it over with my other two lawyers and decided to take part in this trial for now. I also asked that the content of my trial be made public as the court battle would only be meaningful if it publicly reveals the falsehood and wickedness of the prosecution's accusations. I suggested that we consider rejecting the trial, but fighting through the court system might be necessary. However, this kind of fight will extend the trial and thus the defendant will have to spend more time in detention, which is burdensome. And so, our planning has begun.
>
> The arrest warrant will soon expire. However, the judge may issue another warrant to keep me in prison. I continue to look forward to the day that I'm free again, but I know that I don't have the

power to do anything as this is in God's hands. I'm embracing each day because I could have died already. I treat the rest of my life as a bonus.

August 7: Cloudy, "A Whistle Stop of Life"

Writer Hwang Dae Gwon and his son Aram came to see me yesterday. I was humbled that he had come to visit me. Hwang often mentioned that he felt a bit distant from his son, however Aram had come with him to join the annual Grand March against the naval base in Gangjeong, and Hwang said he had begun to feel a stronger bond growing between them. I had heard that he delivered a speech to the villagers and marchers at the start of this year's Gangjeong Grand March for Peace and Life.

It was a great pleasure to see them both. His son, Aram, is a tall, handsome young man. His father was unjustly imprisoned for thirteen years during Aram's youth. How much confusion and resentment might he have towards this absent father? How lonely was the son of this father, a person who went away following his own convictions? Gangjeong is a place with many similar sad threads and tangled knots. There are sons full of joy to be re-united with lost fathers, and sons who must watch their fathers leave for prison. Gangjeong has become a whistle stop where loved ones come and go, a way station to and from those they love.

Everyone in jail tries to hide their pasts and identities. However, when you are sharing a tiny prison cell for twenty-four hours-a-day, sooner or later who you are comes out. In the cell, life stories are like the scattered pieces of a puzzle. No one talks about their life as if they are writing an autobiography, rather lives are relayed non-linearly, a series of short stories, told here and there. Many of these stories are dark, grim, and miserable, filled with frustration and disappointment, separation and abandonment, anger and longing, about lives that have gone off track or fallen over the precipice. Ordinary people you meet outside of prison also have various stories of life, but I suspect that most of them aren't as colorful and memorable as the ones in here. Funerals confirms such suspicions. Deaths where no one is particularly upset, where no one really desires to reminisce on the life of the one who has died. These people chase after normal, stable lives like everyone around them, and thus when they die, they die like everyone around them. Others live more unusual lives due to something catastrophic in their environment or unfortunate circumstances beyond their control. Still others choose to carve out their own destiny and path and create a widely varied life of ups and downs. There was a dream I had when I was a teenager. I wanted to create a small library called, "Who!" which would contain autobiographical stories of the various people who live in this world, organized by name. I had a variety of dreams back then and this was just one of them, but even now at my current age, I still keep this dream in the corner of my memory.

August 7: "A Life of Endless Defeat"

I read a little bit of the New Testament in the original Greek every morning. It also has an English comparison translation so I can understand it without a dictionary. Today, was Matthew 26:26, the part about

Jesus' Last Supper. I'm not sure why but I teared up thinking about him sharing his last meal with his disciples of 3 years. Leonardo da Vinci painted the Last Supper within the elegant hall of a fifteenth-century Italian noble family. However, the actual Last Supper would have been a simple meal of unleavened bread and wine on a simple table in a dark, dingy place, like a prison cell. A meal marked by the sadness of something never to be shared again in the world. I'm not sure why, but this last meal with loved ones filled my heart with mourning.

Similarly, Bonhoeffer's prison letters, especially the ones that he wrote reminiscing the loved ones, also broke my heart. Bonhoeffer's happiest memories, when he had spent precious time together with his loved ones on Easter and birthdays, had all become a thing of the past. In his letters, he wondered whether he would ever experience a time of happiness again, or if he was to just be satisfied with those beautiful memories of the past in his current situation.

Bonhoeffer's earnest desire to meet those he loved again was eventually denied. When he returned to his loved ones, he was no longer alive. The history of injustice murdering justice constantly repeats, not only in the time of Christ, but also in Germany in the 1940s, and still now at the beginning of the millennium in Korea. We must learn the hidden truths of history through the lives and deaths of those who were persecuted for their beliefs and faith in Christ and his justice. The meaning of life lies not in victory, but in defeat. We can't withdraw after one or two small defeats, moving back a few steps or losing a few times. To beat back despair and frustration, to overcome all trials, we must infinitely affirm our lives of endless loss. I believe. I believe in the truth that we lose and God is victorious; we die but God will raise us from the dead.

August 12: Sunny, "Refusal of Imprisonment"

This is my last night in my current cell. I spent 130 days here. I've decided to refuse my imprisonment and tomorrow I will have my inmate number removed and they will isolate me for interrogation. I am grateful to the inmates in my cell for their friendship. They do not understand why I am doing this. They don't understand why I would give up my comfortable cell leadership position to make life more uncomfortable and inconvenient by rejecting my imprisonment. I am going to refuse my imprisonment, because I am not guilty of anything. I'm not a prisoner. I know I am innocent, and I am going to defend my rights in this prison. My decision will cause a strain on my relationship with the prison guards. They will think I'm crazy and treat me like I'm delusional. But I will uphold my own dignity. If I don't protect my own dignity who will? I will remove this number 611 attached to my sleeve, and live and act as a free man. If they try to handcuff me or tie me up, I will go on a hunger strike. I would rather die with dignity than live in misery.

August 12: "If My Mind and Soul Were Free"

Dear Jeong Rae,

This may be the last letter I can send you from prison. If I am lucky, they will acknowledge my decision to refuse imprisonment and allow us to keep correspondence. But I do not have much hope for such outcome. From tomorrow, I will act out my freedom in here. Fr. Moon Jeong Hyeon expressed concern about my decision, but I do not think I will change my mind. This will not affect my fellow prisoners Dong Won and Bok Cheol either. I will express my innocence by taking off this prison uniform. I pity myself in this uniform. Therefore, I will take my own side for this poor human being. I'm not guilty and I will declare my innocence. When I was young, I saw a dog get run over by a car. That dog lost a leg. Just as that dog licked its wounds and limped away, I limp here with my shattered dignity.

Does my isolation drive me to compulsion? My fellow cellmates feel sorry that I've lost my mind, that I'm trying to do something insane. The prison warden says he understands my feelings but failing to comply with the prison rules will lead to greater punishment. I feel like I've fallen into some labyrinth, but I will follow the sound of my conscience. I'm sorry. It is likely I won't be able to meet for Saem's birthday, your birthday, or Chuseok. Please tell my father that as I'm imprisoned, I won't be able to spend Chuseok together. Please tell him I'm so sorry. I often think of my parents in here.

I hate being forced to do anything, but if my body is confined and my mind and soul can be free, I can overcome any sadness. If you can't see or contact me for a while, please don't worry too much. God will take care of me. I just hope it's not too long. Goodbye until we can meet again.

On a Sunday evening
Your husband, Song Kang Ho

August 13: "Only for the Sake of Others"

Dear Jeong Rae,

Today, I had a meeting with the Chief Prison Officer and the Prison Warden to discuss my demands. They positively considered my demands and made some arrangements in my favor. I won't be punished or harshly investigated, which means visitations and correspondence will still be permitted. I have also been able to negotiate a mutual understanding with some of the prison guards. I suppose I should put aside the uncertainties of the future and try to solve things one by one. They could have treated me worse, So I'm grateful they are handling my case thoughtfully and with care.

I've transferred into a solitary cell and am now living all by myself. This means that I do not have to have the TV on if I do not feel like it. This silence is an indescribable blessing, I am ecstatic at this gift. It is a tremendous joy to think, pray, and write without being interrupted. Sometimes I even read or sing aloud. My cell is still cramped and hot, and the water doesn't work well, but the benefits I've gained are incomparable. I can once again meet you, Saem, Silver, Emily, SOS, and the Gangjeong villagers. I will wear my prison number then, just to see you, only for the sake of others.

Your husband, Song Kang Ho

August 14: "Innocent Blood"

I moved to a solitary cell yesterday. They have granted me some freedoms and additional considerations. The cell itself is very small, but it has a toilet, and most importantly, it is quiet and free because there are no cellmates blasting the television or endlessly angrily quarrelling. I believe Dong Won and Bok Cheol would very much like a room like this.

Looking through some scrapped articles, I came across an article about the filing of a lawsuit against the U.S. government by the families of Samir Khan and Anwar al-Awlaki and his son Abdulrahman al-Awlaki, who were killed in U.S. drone strikes in Yemen last year. Suddenly a thought flashed through my mind. Maybe even an amazing discovery, perhaps a groundbreaking way to stop war. War always brings innocent civilian victims. Most people ignore this shedding of innocent blood. Others say it's unavoidable, that it's collateral damage. But this is not a righteous justification, and it should not be done. Even if we were to allow the attacking and killing of armed soldiers and enemies as somehow justified, it is still necessary to investigate the deaths of obvious victims such as innocent civilians, children, women, and the elderly. An international organization could verify deaths and injuries and file claims for compensation against the warring states with the International Court of Justice. Ministers of Defense, Presidents, and various military personnel of the war criminal countries could be identified and put on trial. Following the trials, appropriate compensations should be given, the scale of which should be unlimited, so as to be economically burdensome and social legitimate. This is definitely something that needs to be done. This could lead to an agreement to ban weapons of mass destruction such as cluster and nuclear bombs. As these are inhumane weapons that bring the inevitable sacrifice of countless innocents, such cases must be brought to the International Court of Justice. Of course, this will not solve everything but international pressure and consequences for war, as well as compensation for innocent blood could contribute to controlling some of the madness of war, even if just a bit. This is something that must be done. I will do it!

August 20: Sunny, "The Truth We Already Know"

Last Monday, I watched several interesting documentaries. In the morning, I watched a special feature on global warming and renewable energy, and in the afternoon, a report on a water tribe called the Bajau Laut living in north-eastern Borneo. In an intersection of the two documentaries, the evening news contained a report that thousands of fish had died on fish farms on the southern coast of Korea due to the rising water temperatures. As endless human greed destroys the environment and causes temperatures to rise, nature seems to be taking revenge. The production of renewable energy is important, but after seeing that the U.S. is developing renewable energy for military and war use, it seems more important to live a life using less energy of any kind, like the Bajau Laut.

It's a truth we already know: self-sufficiency and self-control. Whaling ships equipped with modern technology can catch more whales and earn more income. But humans can co-exist with whales if we restrict ourselves to traditional whaling methods, like those of the Lamalera people of Flores, Indonesia. Similarly, our oceans would be once again filled with big fish like tuna if modern ocean vessels with huge freezers were banned and fishing had to be done in traditional Bajau style. Do you know that such a culture of marine restraint and self-sufficiency already exists in Korea? Our chief example is Jeju's traditional female divers. If you were to utilize well-equipped professional divers, you might gather more in a shorter time and earn more money. But that would not be sustainable. We need to control our infinite human greed more than we need to produce alternative energy. That's the priority. You should learn why peace activist Gandhi spun his wheel. You should learn why all he left behind when he died was a pair of round glasses and a pair of rubber shoes.

In a tiny room like a prison cell, people will try to make the most efficient use of their given space. Is there any other animal in the world that lives like humans, building huge rooms and houses? War often comes from expansion, so if we let go of our greed, what use will we have for war? The discovery of oil and gas started Japan and China fighting over the Senkaku Islands, and six or seven neighboring countries arguing over the Spratly Islands. Wars over oil continue in Iraq and Afghanistan. If humanity decided to live without electricity like the Amish, then there would be no need for countries to fight for depleted natural resources. Perhaps the peace movement needs to follow a new path of life through a return to traditional self-sufficiency and self-restraint.

August 31: Clear blue sky, "A World without War"

Late summer has a glow about it. After two typhoons, Jeju's sky is now a deep blue. The intense and all-encompassing sunlight creates a dry, cool feel. I had a video visitation from Jung Ae. She told me about preparations for inviting people to the next peace camp. Soon after, I met with one of my lawyers, Baek Shin Ok. She told me that she had applied for a bail release for me, but I told her I didn't want to beg for release and did not want to make any kind of deposit or guarantee.

I don't eat lunch these days. Sometimes I just drink a soy milk or eat an apple and skip the rest. I want to feel hungry at least once a day. It's my pseudo-yin-yang theory. Just as the harmony of light and dark brings comfort to the eyes, a harmony of fullness and hunger makes my stomach at peace. It's like taking a rest after hard exercise. So anyway, I don't have enough energy this afternoon.

Today is the last day of August, which means I have spent five months in prison. I might have to occupy this cell for another month or so. Sometimes this room feels like a cave, and other times it feels as if I am inside the belly of Jonah's big fish. Of course, there is no guarantee that I will be released in the next couple of months, but I believe there is a good chance. I have faith that good things will happen. Until then, I will continue to use this experience to further train my mind and body. My forced simple life allows me to gain as much as I've lost. Time is the main thing. Time is seldom interrupted by trivial matters. It can be very monotonous but with good time management you can enjoy reading, writing, praying, and meditating. I also watch TV and sometimes I play Janggi(Chinese Chess) by myself on the weekends. That's probably the only entertainment I have here. During the day, I get one hour to exercise outside per day.

As this is the only time I can get out of this narrow cell, I run mindlessly around the small roofless prison yard. Even if it rains, I run like any other day, so some of the other inmates think I've lost my mind.

I read a novel titled *The Night Sings* written by Kim Yeon Su. It was about the sad history of those who fought for independence and freedom from Japanese colonial rule in Jiandao. They were betrayed by their own comrades and executed. Their stories are just one of many tragedies during the some of the darkest times of Korean history. Time just passed, turning a blind eye to these lullabies of pain that filled long, long nights. Countless men and women lived passionately without giving up hope, but eventually died in misery and pain. If they had given up that hope, they might have been able to live a normal life like everyone else, but they couldn't. They spent their life fighting against the oppressive Japanese empire until their youthful faces turned wrinkled and their hair gray. They must have been possessed.

Perhaps, I too, am possessed. That must be why a fifty-something-year-old has found himself trapped in a dark solitary cell. If I didn't know the hope for peace, I might have led a comfortable life, but peace has been a disaster. If I, like most people, simply responded reflexively to war without any particular convictions, either running away from war or marching towards it, perhaps I wouldn't be sitting in this prison cell. But I'm cursed to dream of a world without war. I am sorrowfully happy that this disaster and curse has been placed on me. Have you every cried tears of joy? Longing for peace is both my curse and the joy of my salvation. I dream of a world without war from a tiny solitary room. I dream of breaking up the multi-trillion-dollar industry of defense and weaponry and use that money for medical and educational purposes. To create a world where people losing legs to landmines is seen as barbarism and no longer tolerated. I dream of a world where we no longer hear reports of the deaths of 100,000 soldiers and two million civilian victims. My cursed conviction is the hope for a future where weapons and military uniforms can only be found in museums.

I bow my head to Jesus Christ and the prophets of God who give me this faith and hope. I will continue their legacy. It's not up to me whether the world changes or not. My role and mission are to take this dream and spread it deep and wide. The time when there is no more war or soldiers or military bases is in the hands of God, it's not up to me. My job is to make every effort that I can to create a path out of this violence of our generation, in hopes that others might take that path.

September 7: "An Invisible Community in Gangjeong Village"

I re-read an article about the Peace March in Hiroshima. In the pictures, the smiling face of Gangjeong villager Jeong Young Hee and her bright yellow Gangjeong t-shirt caught my eye. She looked like a middle-aged man after shaving her head in protest in Gangjeong. I can only imagine how she must have poured her heart into the testimony as about a thousand women from all around the world responded to her appeal for help with a standing ovation. Tears filled my eyes.

Sitting absent-mindedly in my narrow cell, the faces of various people rushing around to protect Gangjeong village and Gureombi came to mind. Fr. Moon Jeong Hyeon fell through a deep gap between concrete breakwater tetrapods being knocked down during confrontation with the violent police interrupting holy mass. Dong Won climbed up a barge crane. Koh Kwon Il sat alone atop a watchtower. Many women sit daily in front of the main construction gate and are dragged across the pavement by police. Fr. Kim Seong Han, Rev. Jeong Yeon Gil, Seok Jin, Young Jae, and Yong hung an antibase banner from the top of an enormous barge and were dragged down. Sung Hee tirelessly works to inform the peace activists of the world about the Gangjeong struggle. Yoon Mo continues to hold one-person demonstrations at the gates despite his poor health. Jong Hwan continues to prepare meals for the protestors. Familiar faces protest in front of the World Conservation Congress despite government's scorns. The elderly residents of Gangjeong travel the island pleading for help. Their faces and such images flash through my mind, one by one.

No one person is in charge, but like a flock of geese flying in formation, the villagers and peacekeepers of Gangjeong are united together in our search for that far-off land of peace. They will feed you when you are hungry. They will lend you their shoulders to cry on when your heart is weary. They will give you a place to lay your head when you are exhausted. The people of peace who have come to this village to prevent the construction of a naval base in Gangjeong village make peace, live in vibrant community without borders or rules. Experiencing this new community brimming with freedom and life, I realize that perhaps community is not best created by rules or creeds but by its capacity for justice and peace. I have always told younger colleagues that a community should be guided by a vision not a person. I feel like I'm finally realizing the true meaning of what I've always claimed.

Peace is the vision of The Frontiers. Our vision is a peaceful world without war, military bases, armies, and soldiers. This the dream of 3,000 years of faithful believers, from the ancient prophets to the early church, to reformation and onward. The form of community practiced by The Frontiers is only a temporary tool to realize this vision. Therefore, its form and framework must be flexible and malleable. The goal of a community should never be its own survival. Let's not stick stubbornly to our own ways of making peace but let our vision of peace lead us as it may. The Frontiers exist for peace, peace does not exist for the survival of The Frontiers. When this order is forgotten, a community becomes isolated and fossilized, leading to self-destruction.

Chapter 13

Man Named Song Kang Ho

By Song Han Byeol

Dear Father,

It's already been a month since your freedom was taken away in the name of the law. You may not believe this, but not a single day has passed without me thinking of you. To think hard and being angry about why you have been arrested and are forced to stay inside a prison cell is an assignment given to us remaining on the outside. Not only as a father's son, but also as one of those on the outside and free, I lament myself in pain.

Before I begin to study, I start my day by reading an article by Dr. Jang Ki Ryeo. He is like a mentor, and I often use his life as a guide. His life was ahead of his time, and really touches me and gives me courage. Like you, he has lived his life for peace. Some of his writings remind me of you.

"I cancelled everything in Seoul and returned to Busan on April 17, 1973, to help sort out internal issues at the Gospel Hospital in Busan. I was originally scheduled to attend a lecture at the surgical clinic on the 17th, a picnic with friends on the 18th, a surgical examination on the 19th, a baptism on the 21st, a church memorial ceremony on the 22nd, a meeting with a friend on the 23rd, a tennis match in the morning and a church convention in the afternoon of the 24th, and a trip to Busan on the 25th. However, when I heard that there was a dispute between employees at Gospel Hospital in Busan, I immediately dropped everything and went there directly. This is the first time I can remember cancelling all lectures, appointments, and church commitments at once. However, it was clear that I had to prioritize my responsibility as head director of Gospel Hospital. Some might question if my responsibly as hospital director was really that important, but I believe that work is, without question, an important responsibility and the mission that God has given me. My mission of working for peace in the hospital has been and will always be my first priority in life, so I had no choice to but to set aside my other responsibilities.

Working for peace is just that important. Everything else falls to the wayside. It is so important that this was why our Lord came to this world and will return again. Our Lord came to us with the divine responsibility to save all of humanity by making his peace available to all that needed and yearned for it. He will surely come again to bring world peace once and for all because he knows it is the most important thing in the world and his greatest responsibility."

"While the majority of people throughout history have allowed themselves to be passively swept away by the currents of their times, there have been a few who have stuck to their ideals and sounded a warning against the realities to come. They are the men of faith who could discern right from wrong because they were able to see far back and far ahead, not just what lay right in front of them. The world ignores them and tries to destroy them. However, as time passes, and the wrongs are inevitably revealed and the rights acknowledged, such people are vindicated and exalted."[12]

Father, as I've told you before, in my short life, you are the one I've observed more closely than anyone else. My trust in people is rooted in you. When I was younger, I used to fear that one day you might just give up on your faith in peace and live a different way, and if that had happened, I might have had difficulty maintaining my trust in people. I no longer have such doubts.

I sometimes can be conceited, thinking that I am a good and smart person. But there are times when you come across people whose lives are so incredibly awe-inspiring, you wonder, "How is such a life possible?" George Washington Carver is one such person. A black man, born and raised in slavery, he suffered abuse and discrimination, but chose to love even those who hated him. Similarly, my questions about life found answers through the lives

---

12 Yeo Woon Hak, *Life and Love*.

of people like Kim Koo, who loved our people dearly, Gandhi the pacifist, Albert Schweitzer who taught me the real value of life, and Jeon Tae Il who chose to die for his fellow workers in the labor movement. These people helped me to see that no matter how evil the world is, no matter how much people oppress others, no matter how much justice and peace are dismissed as naive fantasies, people like these will appear as the beacons of human history. They arise from the land that is seized by injustice and where people are bound by evil, and they show the world what the life of the "Son of Man" truly was. They teach ordinary people how to hope for more. From them we know justice and peace, which are now mocked and tossed on the street, and finally its value in history will be revealed.

Those who thirst for justice and have fixed their purpose for that fight, may eventually give up their lives. They are willing to sacrifice because of those who have come before. The same goes for the man named Song Kang Ho. You hold in common a sincere life of seeking to uphold the most precious values that resonate from within you. Although you may bleed for it, your resilience and perseverance hold even those that hate you in awe. Father, you are surely such a person.

You were violently assaulted and arrested on your birthday. I wanted to tell you something that day but couldn't. If that day hadn't happened, the world would be poorer for it. The value of a person's life is not just how they lived it, but also how those who gather round them live. Your life has been an inspiration for many people. They may not be great in number, but they are the living proof of your life's purpose for peace. I am proud to be one of them.

How would life be different for us now if you had not existed? If Saem had been born into an ordinary family, she might be just a regular self-focused pretty woman. I probably would have become some sort of smart but impersonal scientist. Mom would have probably lived as her gentle self with a nice family. I think uncle Hyung Woo and uncle Kwang Il would be hard-working family men. I guess uncle Chul would have been a farmer or a carpenter. And what about the rest of The Frontiers and all those Gangjeong residents? One thing is sure, if you hadn't been my father, I would never have had the dream that I have now.

Studying medicine is a challenging journey, and I admit that I'm often exhausted and drained. However, what I find more challenging is finding peers who share the same dream and values that I do. It makes me sad when they view Dr. Jang Ki Ryeo as a naive dreamer. When I run into my own weaknesses, I think to myself how this dream of emulating Dr. Jang Ki Ryeo is just too much for me. I get very lonely and empty. In a TV show called "Behind the White Tower," there is a scene where a medical doctor asks one of his students: "Do you know why this work is so difficult? It's because you're on the right path. I believe this is a beautiful road. In this world, we need more of those who are willing to walk the right path for whatever it may take."

It is true that this path is sometimes overwhelming. Although studying and practicing medicine every day is a challenge, the fact that my life may one day become a beacon of hope for someone in the future keeps me going. You have been that hope. You are the one who invited me to live such a wondrous life. Please keep your lacking son in your prayers.

My excuse for delaying writing to you is that I had to overcome my own grief and shame to be ready to write to you. Father, on your lonely road ahead, remember that there are many people, who hold you as their inspiration. I, Han Byeol, am one of them. In my mind, I can see, clearer than ever, the wings of freedom reaching out to the sky above Jeju Prison in Ora 2-dong.

Sincerely,
Your son, Han Byeol
Mid-May 2012

"Oh, Gangjeong, you are the smallest town in this land, but the peace of every nation shall begin with you."

Voyage Towards Peace

A 3,000-Year-Old Dream

In a sense, everyone lives on their own island. That island is shaped by the memories of the people they love. There may be conflicts and disagreements, but they mostly live at peace on their island. These islands can be small, including just a family, or they can be very large, containing big communities or nations. Regardless, outside the boundaries of that island, lies what looks like a great, cold sea of indifference. The voyage towards peace between islands starts by pushing a boat out onto that rough sea. You will have to battle storms and rough seas. The boat may capsize or break in the middle of the vast ocean. The path to peace is never safe. But there is something more dangerous than rough waves, and that is when there is no wind. There is nothing as dangerous for a small sailboat than being unable to move, stuck and isolated. Imagine a sailboat that is trapped in the middle of a windless sea. Some mistake such a situation for safety. Yet, while a boat can sail even against a headwind, a boat on still water cannot go anywhere and such areas are only filled with dead fish and the garbage washed up there by ocean currents.

God formed humanity from the dust of the earth and breathed life into us. On the sea, the winds of life blow us on our voyage towards peace. The hope and passion for peace beyond the borders formed in blood, the boundaries of family and ethnicity, is a spiritual wind blowing from the Kingdom of God. Fortunately, I was not born in the Roman Empire or during the Joseon Dynasty, so I have not been persecuted merely for believing in Jesus. But when I tried to practice the peace of the prophets and the peace taught by Jesus Christ, the church rejected me, and the state imprisoned me. I am punished for following the declarations of the prophets Isaiah and Micah, "They will beat their swords into plowshares and their spears into pruning hooks. Nation will not take up sword against nation, nor will they train for war anymore." (Isaiah 2:4, Micah 4:3). Moreover, this is the price of obeying Jesus Christ when he taught us to "Love your neighbor as yourself" (Matthew 19:19) and warned us, "Put your sword back in its place, for all who draw the sword will die by the sword" (Matthew 26:52).

In our generation, the church and state allow people to believe in Christ but does not allow them to practice His teachings. I reject this contradiction. The church denies its own peace traditions, embedded in our faith from the lessons of the prophets through the teachings of Jesus Christ. It also hides the history of anti-war peace values which the early church upheld at the expense of their lives. The state engages in war for the sake of greedy national interest, for a people mired in collective selfishness. Korea exports weapons of mass destruction to foreign countries, using blood money to fill the stomachs of our people.

Only through God's grace can I live my life surrounded by threats in this age of lies. I partake in the magnificent 3,000-year dream of peace that the prophets, Jesus Christ and the forefathers of our faith dreamed of. And I join them in the suffering they experienced. This dream is not like that of the farmer who plants in the spring and harvests in the fall. It's not an investment you make for retirement when you are still young. The realization of this dream may be in the distant future. Countless people before us have desperately dreamed this dream in pain and sorrow for thousands of years. One who dreams of a world without war, militaries, and weapons will surely look like a madman. A person who is addicted to this dream falls into a happy hallucination. It is a surreal experience only those who are preoccupied by the future will feel. It is a bit like the hallucinations of the drug addict. A peace addiction can be comparable to drug addiction, but they are different. Where drug addiction paralyses and destroys the body, and disconnect relationships, peace inspires us with its prophetic imagination, develops our artistic sensibilities, and allows us to make true friends who will support us through hardship and share our thirst for justice and peace. "Blessed are the peacemakers, for they will be called children of God" (Matthew 5:9). These words can be realized when one dedicates oneself to peace. Truly, peace makes us happy.

I hope that you will all dedicate your lives to peace. I hope the young people lining up nervously for job interviews during this recession will instead boldly rip up their application forms and become full-time peace activists. Seeking employment is a bloody competition, a red ocean. In contrast there are very few people looking to plunge into the blue ocean of peace work. When I first started down this path, I was prepared to beg for my subsistence. I assumed that it would be difficult to survive. But those who live for justice and peace do not go hungry. Peacemakers are the ambassadors of God's Kingdom and God still provides his servants with manna and quail.

Letter of Invitation

I invite you all to Gangjeong village. Gangjeong is lonely. Even the residents of Hwasun and Wimi, who once resisted the construction of the naval base in their own towns, now turn a blind eye to the residents of Gangjeong. Hwasun residents have even allowed their port to manufacture caissons for the construction of the Gangjeong Naval Base. Of course, it's all for profit. The residents of Gangjeong are unable to say anything about this, for in the past, when Hwasun and Wimi fought tooth and nail with bamboo spears in opposition to the naval base in their areas, Gangjeong merely looked on, as if it was someone else's problem. However, now the flames that burned across the river have moved to Gangjeong. Swallowing their pride, Gangjeong residents travel round and round till their feet ache, appealing to the people of Jeju Island. Maybe it's true they have no right to ask for help now. But if you've ever received a favor that you didn't deserve, perhaps you could help these lonely villagers.

I am still fighting to prevent the construction of this destructive war base and to instead create a peace park on the sacred rock of Gureombi. I dream that people of peace will cross the cloud-covered Mt. Halla towards the sea-drenched horizon and gather on Gureombi in Gangjeong village. Gangjeong is a school that will teach you peace through fighting the evil spirits of war and violence. Here in Gangjeong, I watch young people grow to be workers in the Kingdom of God's peace through this beautiful struggle. These young people who have learned peace here will one day sow peace in conflicts around the world. Gangjeong is a seedbed for nurturing these seeds of peace.

Not only Gangjeong, but many islands around the world have been turned or are being turned into military facilities. The United States, China and Japan are trying to build military facilities across the Pacific, Indian Ocean, and South China Sea. Many of these islands are isolated and have small populations, so even if the residents are forcefully displaced, there is little attention from the international community.13 This is why the U.S. took the island of Oahu and built Pearl Harbor. The residents of Diego Garcia and Okinawa were also forced to move for U.S. Military bases. The U.S. has then used such bases as springboards to start and maintain wars in Vietnam, the Persian Gulf, and Afghanistan, resulting in millions of civilian deaths. Meanwhile China seeks to establish a naval base on the Spratly Islands so as to secure its claims to the nearby oil fields. Japan seeks to establish a Self-Defense Force base on the small island of Yonaguni near the border of Taiwan, as part of their struggle to secure control of the Senkaku Islands against China. Our struggle against the naval base on Jeju Island should join in solidarity with the islanders of Hawaii, Okinawa, Yonaguni, and Diego Garcia, as our struggle and suffering are one. We must develop an international demilitarized peace island

---

13 Professor David Vine argues that this is the reason the U.S. has been developing its Strategic Island Concept around the world since World War II. See David Vine, *Island of Shame* (New Jersey: Princeton University Press, 2009), p.4.

movement to protect and link the many islands scattered across the oceans of the world. Islanders should never again suffer the nightmare of militaries rushing in to confiscate their land and remove them from their peaceful homes. Think of Pearl Harbor. Pearl Harbor is so contaminated by the heavy metals of its naval base that its waters no longer have any pearls. The sea is a blue continent shared by humanity. No one should use our seas and islands as an oasis for war.

The Republic of Korea government and its navy believe that they can sacrifice the tiny Gangjeong village for their military interests. Gangjeong villagers have been betrayed by their own country and left to suffer in silence. Why must Gangjeong village suffer such pain? Is this merely the pain of birthing an unwanted naval base, coerced through state violence? I don't think so. I think these are the birth pangs of Gangjeong's rebirth as a port of peace. Gangjeong will be a place that cultivates peace warriors who dream of a world without war. And it will be blessed to send those warriors to islands in danger around the world. And Gureombi will become a park of life and peace that people from all over the world will come to, to sing, dance, learn and teach peace. Let's dream! The 3,000-year-old dream of peace. A world without slaves or masters, a world without aristocrats or commoners, a world where genders are equal, and a world where people are not discriminated against for the color of their skin. All these used to be naive dreams. I believe that one day a world without war and a world without soldiers will be within reach. There is no impossible dream in the world. It's only for lack of people willing to embrace this dream together. The more of us that embrace this dream, the closer it comes to reality.

A dream of peace is only a dream until you decide to sail for peace. Get on board! Let's sail through the deep blue sea of peace! Remember, the more dangerous a place, the more beautiful it is. A life lived for peace shows us the desperate hell that is our current reality, but at the same time, it will show us how beautiful and brilliant life can be. I invite you to the most beautiful voyage in the world.

From Jeju Prison, beneath Geomun Oreum at the foothills of Mt. Halla,
Song Kang Ho
September 7, 2012

"Oh, Gangjeong, you are the smallest town in this land, but the peace of every nation shall begin with you."
-Bishop Kang Woo Il, from his sermon

APPENDIX

Jeju Island and Gangjeong Village Timeline
2002 – October 2022

2002
- UNESCO designates Jeju Island as a Biosphere Reserve
- Ministry of Oceans and Fisheries announces Second Coastal Port Master Plan (Including Naval Dock Construction in Hwasoon Port, Jeju)
- Jeju Island releases an Official Statement of Opposition to the Construction of Hwasoon Port Naval Dock
- Democratic Party presidential candidate, Roh Moo Hyun promises full review of the Hwasoon Port Project

2004
- Jeju Island designates Gangjeong Coast as an Absolute Preservation Area (Article 292 Paragraph 3, Jeju Island Special Act)

2005
- ROK Government designates Jeju Island as "Island of World Peace"
- Jeju Governor Kim Tae Hwan announces suspension of discussions regarding the construction of naval base in Hwasoon Port

2006
- ROK Defense Acquisition Program Administration announces the policy of enforcement for the naval base construction
- Catholic Diocese of Jeju declares opposition to naval base construction
- UNESCO lists Jeju Island as a World Natural Heritage Site

February 2007
- Prime Minister Han Myeong Sook responds to the National Assembly that Jeju Naval Base is necessary for military strategy.

April 2007
- Gangjeong Mayor Yoon Tae Jeong convenes an unplanned general meeting (87 villagers participating). The participants affirm to host the naval base via clapping. The meeting violated village governance regulations: obligation to announce general meetings with proper advance notice, obligation to broadcast meeting announcement frequently, obligation to provide appropriate notice.

May 2007
- Naval Base Construction Project Group conducts project briefing session and public opinion poll
- Jeju Governor Kim Tae Hwan announces the decision to invite naval base to Gangjeong village
- Gangjeong Villagers' Committee to Stop the Naval Base launched.

June
- Jeju Island Provincial Assembly raises the issue that Naval Base Construction Project Group manipulated public opinion polls

July
- Gangjeong Village Emergency General Meeting: Mayor Yoon Tae Jeong, who was in charge of hosting the naval base, dismissed. New mayor Kang Dong Gyun elected
- Jeju Branch of Korean Federation for Environmental Movements discovers a large population of endangered Clithon retropictus near Gangjeong Port

- Jeju Provincial Audit Committee announces audit results of naval base public opinion poll. The results show that administrative procedures were ignored, and "Local Government Act" violated

August
- Gangjeong Village Referendum on the naval base issue conducted: 725 out of the total 1,050 villagers participate (69%); 680 voters oppose the naval base construction (94%)

September 2008
- ROK Prime Minister's Office officially names Jeju naval base. Korean name translation: "Civilian-Military Combination Tourism Beauty Port"; Official English name: "Jeju Civilian-Military Complex Port"

November
- Green Korea observes several endangered species including orange cup coral and Triton's trumpet sea snail, along the coastline of Gangjeong village

January 2009
- ROK Ministry of National Defense announces the approval of Defense and Military Facility Project Implementation Plan
- Gangjeong village files a lawsuit, "Confirmation of Invalidation of Approval of Defense and Military Facility Project Implementation Plan"

February
- Joint ecosystem survey by pro and anti-base villagers discovers legally protected soft coral colonies, including Alcyonium gracillimum Kükenthal and antipathies japonica

July
- ROK Ministry of National Defense selects Samsung C&T and Daelim E&C Consortium as qualified port construction companies

December
- Jeju Provincial Assembly hastily cancels Gangjeong's status as an Absolute Preservation Area

January 2010
- Gangjeong village files a lawsuit "Suspension and Invalidation for the Absolute Preservation Area Change Disposition"

March
- Seoul Administrative Court rules against Gangjeong's lawsuit, "Confirmation of Invalidation of Approval of Defense and Military Facility Project Implementation Plan"

April
- Gangjeong village files a lawsuit, "Approval of Public Water Reclamation"

November
- Jeju Provincial Governor Woo Geun Min announces the official acceptance of Naval Base Project in Gangjeong

December
- ROK National Assembly passes 2011 budget that includes the construction budget for Jeju Naval Base
- Jeju District Court dismisses Gangjeong village's lawsuit, "Suspension and Invalidation for the Absolute Preservation Area Change Disposition" on the grounds that "residents involved are not qualified to be plaintiffs"

February 2011
- Construction of the Jeju Naval Base begins

March
- Jeju Provincial Assembly decides to reverse the cancelation of Absolute Preservation Area designation

April
- Film director Yang Yoon Mo is arrested and imprisoned on charge of Obstruction of Business. He goes on a hunger strike in prison.

May
- Jeju District Court dismisses the second appeal against "Revocation of Absolute Preservation Area"
- Jeju District Court rejects the "Application for injunction of Suspension of Outdoor Assembly and Demonstration" lawsuit
- Five Opposition Party Fact-finding Mission Group (Democratic Party, Democratic Labor Party, Creative Korea Party, New Progressive Party, People Participation Party) visit Jeju Island and protest

June
- Yang Yoon Mo is released on probation

July
- Launch of 1st National Citizens' Action for Cancellation of Jeju Naval Base
- 25 progressive American intellectuals, including Prof. Noam Chomsky, issue statement against the Jeju Naval Base
- Police arrest Gangjeong Mayor Kang Dong Gyun, Gangjeong Anti-Base Committee Chairman Koh Kwon Il, and Dr. Song Kang Ho
- "Civilian Peace Action to Defend Gangjeong and Cancel the Jeju Naval Base Construction" held at Daehanmun Gate in Seoul
- Large-scale police operation deployed in Gangjeong village
- Gangjeong villagers start nightly candlelight vigil at naval base construction office entrance
- Catholic priests and Gangjeong residents begin sit-in tent protests
- Hyeon Ae Ja, Chair of Jeju Provincial Democratic Labor Party and Gangjeong residents begin protesting with metal chains wrapped around their bodies
- Song Kang Ho and Koh Kwon Il are released on probation

© Jindalae Sancheon
His unwavering hope glides him like the sea breeze in search of justice. He has always been a sailor.

© Jindalae Sancheon
He prayed aloud every morning on Gureombi. Even after the path to Gureombi was blocked by fence and barbed wire, he would go there from the sea by kayak. When kayak was not possible, he would swim. Above all else, 'warrior' Song Kang Ho was a person of prayer.

August
- Gangjeong village starts "Anti-Naval Base Construction Cultural Festival" protests
- 600 people participate in "Gangjeong Peace Gathering to Cancel the Naval Base Project"
- Cranes illegally brought to the village; Gangjeong Mayor Kang Dong Gyun and Kim Dong Won are arrested for Obstruction of Business
- Additional large-scale riot police force deployed in Gangjeong Village (16 police buses, 3 water cannons, around 10 special protest suppressor vehicles, 600 mainland police)
- CNN Special Report on Gangjeong village
- Coalition of Pyeongtaek Daechuri, Maehyangri, and Okinawa Residents release the joint statement, "Gangjeong Declaration on Anti-war Solidarity for Peace"

September
- First large-scale police crackdown operation on Gangjeong village protestors
- Navy blocks access to Joongdeok Coast and Gureombi
- KBS TV Program "Chujeok 60 Minutes" airs "Peace Stolen for Economic Logic (The Problem of the Jeju Naval Base)" episode
- Gangjeong holds Peace Concert; 1st batch of "Peace Plane" and "Peace Bus" arrive
- Kim Chan, new director of Cultural Heritage Administration, announces plan to preserve Gangjeong's cultural assets
- Democratic Party resolves to conduct close examination of cultural assets on the naval base construction site
- Korea Council of Christian Churches (KNCC) begins Gangjeong Village Prayer Meeting
- 375 members from "The Emergency Council for Jeju Naval Base Conflict Resolution" announce a peace declaration: "We must totally protect Jeju, the Island of Life and Peace."

October
- Navy physically assaults Song Kang Ho in water. The incident reported on by "Newstapa"
- Police arrest 10 residents and activists protesting against the test demolition of

Gureombi
- Launch of the "Catholic Solidarity for the Realization of Jeju, the Island of Peace"

November
- Catholic Priests' Association for Justice begins hunger strike in front of the National Assembly calling for budget cuts to the Jeju Naval Base
- Gangjeong Village Anti-Base Committee and National Anti-Base Committee submit an opinion on naval base budget cuts to National Assembly

December
- ROK National Assembly cuts 96% of the 2012 naval base construction budget due to the base design errors and unused budget surplus in the 2011 naval base construction budget

January 2012
- Cultural Heritage Administration leads experts' review on the excavation and investigation of cultural assets on the site of Gangjeong Naval Base. Hwang Pyeong Woo, Director of Korean Cultural Heritage Policy Research Institute states, "The construction should be suspended, and a full investigation should be conducted."

February
- ROK Prime Minister's Office's "Technical Verification Committee on Cruise Ship Entry and Departure of the Jeju Civilian-Military Complex Port" admits, "It is difficult for a 150,000-ton cruise ship to enter and exit freely with the navy's port design."
- ROK Ministry of National Defense refutes Technical Verification Committee's report claiming that the current design has no errors and guarantees use by cruise ships
- Film Director Yang Yoon Mo incarcerated again and starts second hunger strike
- ROK National Intelligence Service raids SPARK(Solidarity for Peace and Reunification in Korea) officers for search and seizure on charges of violating the National Security Act

- ROK President Lee Myung Bak announces "Jeju Naval Base construction enforcement" at a special press conference on the 4th anniversary of his inauguration.
- Bruce Cummings, Professor at the University of Chicago, claims in Oh My News interview, "If Sino-American war breaks out over Taiwan, the U.S. will put into use the Jeju Naval Base for their war."

March
- The Navy and Samsung C&T enforce the blasting demolition of Gureombi Rock
- Jeju Provincial Assembly gives report on urgent issues related to the Jeju Civilian-Military Complex Port
- Jeju Provincial Assembly Administration and Home Affairs Committee visit to the naval base blocked by the navy
- Jeju Island holds a hearing following the suspension of public water reclamation work
- Jeju Provincial Assembly refuses port design verification meeting and announces position on the enforcement of construction.
- Gangjeong village refuses port design verification meeting and demands suspension of construction
- Yang Yoon Mo is released on bail following 42-day hunger strike

April
- ROK Prime Minister's Office conducts a verification meeting on the port design simulation results
- Song Kang Ho is arrested again for Obstruction of Business (2nd imprisonment)

May
- Jeju District Court dismisses plaintiff's claim for revocation of approval disposition for reclamation of public waters (1st trial)

June
- 'SKY ACT' is launched to bring solidarity between and resolve the problems of Ssangyong Motors workers, Gureombi/Gangjeong and the Yongsan disasters.

July
- ROK Supreme Court rules that "Approval of Defense and Military Facility Project Implementation Plan" is legal
- SKY ACT's joint nationwide anti-naval base tour launched
- Korean church representatives hold a prayer rally for Song's release
- On the 100th day of Song's arrest, country-wide one-person protests call for his release
- Gangjeong Grand March for Life and Peace across Jeju Island held July 31 – August 4 with around 7,000 participants

August
- ROK National Assembly holds discussion on viability of the Jeju Naval Base
- National Citizens' Action holds 13th nationwide rally to cancel the Jeju Naval Base

September
- Global & Asia Pacific Greens Network organizes "International Anti-Jeju Naval Base Action Week" from September 2-9
- The International Union for Conservation of Nature (IUCN) holds their World Conservation Congress (WCC) in Jeju Island
- Democratic United Party Rep. Jang Hana claims at a National Assembly hearing that Jeju Naval Base being built to the standards of use for U.S. nuclear aircraft carriers
- Jeju court fines barge captain and Samsung C&T for transportation of construction caissons without ship safety inspection
- United Nations Human Rights Council (UNHRC) recommends the Korean government to provide explanation on the violence in Gangjeong village
- Song Kang Ho is released on September 28 on bail after 181 days.

October 2012
- SKTM(Ssangyong, Gangjeong, Yongsan, Milyang) Grand March for Life and Peace

December
- Jeju Buddhists' Association in collaboration with Hwajaeng(Inter-denominational/inter-religious dialogue) Committee of the Jogye Order of

© Jindalae Sancheon
"Asking for the courage to practice justice and realize peace in the face of violence is the sincerest type of prayer."

© Jindalae Sancheon
Every mode of justice all come together to bring about peace.

Korean Buddhism holds "Dragon King Grand Ceremony for Peace and Hope in Gangjeong" under the theme of "We are Neighbors and Family: for Oneness of Gangjeong."
- Gangjeong village declares the beginning of civil disobedience campaign

January 2013
- Gangjeong Village New Year's Sunrise Ceremony for Peace entitled "Human is Universe."
- "Island of Peace" Declaration Ceremony

February
- Official announcement of the approved change in the administrative nature of Gangjeong project: Gangjeong project now classified as a "Joint Military-Civilian Tourist Port Construction Plan" instead of former "Nation Defense Facility Project."
- Film director/critic Yang Yoon Mo placed under court custody (ends up being imprisoned for 18 months)

April
- Gangjeong Peace Bookstore opens

May
- Tent for Surveillance of Illegal Construction of Jeju Naval Base is violently torn down
- Gangjeong Mayor Kang Dong Gyun arrested and confined

June
- UN special rapporteur of human rights visits Gangjeong village

July
- 2nd Gangjeong Grand March for Life and Peace held across Jeju Island
- Song Kang Ho and Brother Park Do Hyun arrested and confined

September
- Inauguration of Gangjeong Business Cooperative for Peace

October
- Kang Bu Eon and Kim Eun Hye arrested and confined

May 2014
- Five residents of Gangjeong participate in the Okinawa Grand March for Peace

July
- 3rd Gangjeong Grand March for Life and Peace held across Jeju Island

August
- International peace gathering, "Sea of Peace" held in Gangjeong

November
- Activists put up a tent to retract military personnel quarters for Jeju Naval Base

January 2015
- Administrative execution takes place at the sit-in site in front of the military personnel quarters of Jeju Naval Base

April
- National Labor Day Demonstration honoring Jeju 4.3 Uprising held at Gangjeong stream stadium

July
- 4th Gangjeong Grand March for Life and Peace held across Jeju Island

September
- Gangjeong St. Francisco Peace Center opens

October
- Gangjeong Village International Peace Bureau awarded Sean MacBride Peace Prize in recognition of the "profound commitment they have demonstrated to peace and social justice."

February 2016
- Jeju Naval Base dedication ceremony

March
- Republic of Korea Navy files an indemnity lawsuit against 5 civic groups (including The Frontiers) and 116 individuals (including Song Kang Ho) involved in anti-naval base movement, demanding 3.45 billion KRW (around 3 million USD) in compensation for damages

April
- The 1st International Peace Film Festival in Gangjeong held

August
- 2016 Gangjeong Grand March for Life and Peace held across Jeju Island

March 2017
- USS Stathem, an Aegis destroyer of the US Navy Pacific Fleet enters Jeju Naval Base

June
- USS Dewey, an Aegis destroyer of the US Navy Pacific Fleet enters port of Jeju Naval Base
- HMCS Winnipeg and HMCS Ottawa, Halifax-class frigates of the Royal Canadian Navy enter port of Jeju Naval Base

July
- 2017 Gangjeong Grand March for Life and Peace held across Jeju Island

August
- USNS Henson, an oceanographic survey ship of the US Navy conducts an underwater survey off the Jeju Naval Base

September
- USS Chief, mine countermeasures ship of the US Navy enters port of the Jeju Naval Base

November
- USS Mississippi, a nuclear-powered submarine of the US Navy Pacific Fleet enters port of the Jeju Naval Base

December
- Republic of Korea Navy (under the leadership of newly elected president Moon Jae In) drops the lawsuit against anti-naval groups and individuals filed in March 2017
- Gangjeong Villagers' Association publishes a white paper entitled "Anti-Jeju Naval Base and Life and Peace Movement"

April 2018
- Victims of violence committed by the Korean military during the Vietnam War visit Gangjeong village

July
- Inter-Island Solidarity for Peace of Sea Camp held in Jeju
- 2018 Gangjeong Grand March for Life and Peace held across Jeju Island

September
- 2018 Asia Peace Education Workshop

October
- Protests against the Republic of Korea 2018 International Fleet Review
- President Moon Jae In visits Gangjeong village

February 2019
- Peace activists in Gangjeong visit Miyako Island in solidarity with anti-US base struggles in Miyako and Okinawa

May
- 3 female activists make statements on their objection to military service on International Conscientious Objectors' Day (May 15th)

July
- 2019 Gangjeong Grand March for Life and Peace held across Jeju Island

September
- Launch of Jonah's Whale, a yacht for voyages of peace

March 2020
- Inception of World Peace University Gangjeong Campus
- Song Kang Ho arrested, confined, and sentenced to two years in prison for cutting open a hole in the fence of the Jeju Naval Base and praying on Gureombi Rock.

October 2021
- Song Kang Ho released on parole

December
- Memorial Ceremony commemorating 84th anniversary of the Nanjing Massacre held in Alddreu Airfield; Alddreu was used by the Japanese military for the bombing of Nanjing in the lead-up to the Nanjing Massacre

July 2022
- Jeju Bike March for Life and Peace held

August
- Gangjeong Peace Center opens

September
- Gureombi Peace Festival held

October
- Villager status of peace activists in Gangjeong reinstated in court

*For updates and more information:
  http://www.SaveJejuNow.org

Author

Song Kang Ho is a peace activist, educator, and theologian. He has dedicated his life to making peace, and as a result has spent most of his time in lands of violence and injustice. He is the founder of The Frontiers, an international peacemaking community based in Korea. With The Frontiers he has served in Rwanda, Bosnia, Somalia, East Timor, Aceh(Indonesia), Kashmir(Pakistan), Haiti, Bangladesh, and Gangjeong(Korea).

He earned degrees from Heidelberg University, Yonsei University, and Presbyterian University and Theological Seminary in the areas of practical theology and educational philosophy. He and his wife, Jeong Rae has together served and lived in The Frontiers community for more than 20 years. They have two children, Han Byeol and Saem.

Translators

Hugh Woonggul Park is a minister of the Uniting Church in Australia, currently serving Thornleigh Uniting Church in Sydney. He and his wife, Yoonhee, came to Australia in 1991 and they have two grown-up children, Jessica and Jason. Hugh has a Music Degree from Hanyang University and a Bachelor of Theology and ThM from United Theological College in Sydney. He is the author of *How to Study English through Korean Language* (Ebeetalk, 2009) and is an aquarium hobbyist.

Paco Michelson is a former member of The Frontiers, Gangjeong Maritime Action Team SOS(Save Our Seas), and Ga ngjeong Village International Team. He is also a video artist. His pursuits include having fun, messing around, seeking justice, living peace, and drinking milk tea.